Roses in Bloom is a testament to what happens when resilience meets purpose. These seven women didn't simply survive divorce; they confronted it, learned from it, and chose to build again. Their honesty about the process is what stands out: the financial realities, the identity shifts, the unexpected moments of clarity that come when life forces you to reset.

What Michaella has created here is more than an anthology; it's a space where truth becomes strength. You can feel the integrity in each story. They don't focus on perfection or arrival, just the steady, determined work of rebuilding a life that still matters.

This is a meaningful read for anyone, man or woman, who is navigating transition or reinvention. It's a reminder that a difficult chapter is not the end of the story, and that what comes next can be stronger, wiser, and more intentional than what came before.

– His Excellency, The Most Honorable Andrew Wilson;
High Commissioner of the Commonwealth of The Bahamas to the Republic of Ghana

Roses in Bloom is a powerful collection that captures what it looks like to rebuild a life from the ground up. Through the voices of seven women, the book explores the deep work of healing—emotionally, spiritually, and financially—after experiencing one of life's most jarring transitions. Each author brings her own perspective, yet their journeys echo a shared truth: growth is possible even in seasons that feel impossible. Instead of presenting polished conclusions, these stories reveal the real process of becoming whole again—the confusion, the self-discovery, the moments of courage, and the gradual return to confidence. The anthology honors the complexity of starting over while shining light on the strength that comes from choosing to rise with intention.

What makes this book especially meaningful is its blend of vulnerability and purpose. These women illustrate how faith, inner work, and a willingness to evolve can transform pain into power. Their testimonies create a space where readers can see themselves, find reassurance, and recognize that difficult chapters can lead to unexpected renewal. Roses in Bloom is an invitation: an invitation to heal, to rediscover one's voice, and to embrace the possibility of a brighter season ahead. Anyone walking through transition—or supporting someone who is—will find both comfort and inspiration in its pages.

– **The Honorable Mario Bowleg;** *Member of Parliament, Garden Hills; Minister of Youth, Sports & Culture; Nassau, N.P., The Bahamas*

There's a conversation Michaella and I had that stays with me: "You can love yourself, but learning to be happy with yourself is another thing." That distinction between loving who you are and actually being at peace alone is what makes this book so necessary.

As coordinator of The Bahamas Bridal Show, I see the fairy-tale beginnings. But I also know real life happens after the wedding. These seven women share what happens when the fairy tale ends and you're forced to write a new story. They don't sugarcoat the financial fears, the lonely nights, or the identity shifts that come with starting over.

What makes this anthology powerful is its honesty about rebuilding. These women learned firsthand to do what I always preach: "pay themselves first," which is to invest in their healing, their future, their dreams, before pouring into everyone else. And in doing so, they transformed from divorced women into #1 bestselling authors. That is the kind of bloom that only comes from deep roots.

Every woman navigating life after divorce needs these stories. They prove that your next chapter can be stronger, wiser, and more beautiful than the one before.

– **Makeva Wallace;** *Coordinator, The Bahamas Bridal Show*

This book is raw, it's transparent, and it's honest. Roses in Bloom invites us into the rare beauty of holding joy and sorrow in the same hands. We don't often give ourselves permission to sit with both, but this anthology reminds us that healing begins when we make room for the full truth of our stories.

What resonated most with me were the moments where the authors shared what it meant to rebuild their lives from the inside out. To learn how to breathe again. To trust that broken seasons can still bloom into something breathtaking.

These seven stories are rooted in God's grace, seven testaments to resilience, courage, and faith. Together, the women become a garden: each offering her own color, fragrance, and revelation.

Roses in Bloom is the revelation; the bold decision to grow again, believe again, and walk in purpose even when life once whispered defeat. Nothing is wasted here, not even the pain.

Thank you, Micahella, for the courage and boldness not only to share your story but also to provide a platform for other women to share and own their moments of bloom!

– **Kerel Pinder;** *Author & Producer*

Roses in Bloom is a moving and empowering work that celebrates resilience, faith and the beauty of living with purpose. The visionary author, Michaella Forbes, a strong, intelligent and resilient woman with impeccable business acumen, draws on her own journey and those of other women who turned challenges, hurt, and disappointment into strength. With a heart devoted to helping others live purposeful lives, she reminds readers that they are fearfully and wonderfully made, capable of rising above adversity.

Through themes such as Beauty for Ashes, Grace in Every Season, and On Eagle Wings, she offers encouragement and wisdom for every stage of life. This book is both a guide and an inspiration, empowering women to embrace their journey and bloom in every season.

– **Na-amah Barker;** *Director, Retail Banking and Small Business, Scotiabank (Bahamas) Ltd*

Bold, brave, resilient, and ready for whatever God has in store! *Roses in Bloom* is a profound collection that speaks to the power of testimony. As an author who knows the healing that flows from pen to paper, I was deeply moved by these women who wrote from their hearts unapologetically. Their candid stories of healing, overcoming, and rising again remind us that God still uses our voices as vessels of victory.

Each chapter reflects the truth of Revelation 12:11—*'And they overcame him by the blood of the Lamb and by the word of their testimony.'* These women have not only survived; they have blossomed, offering hope to every reader who dares to believe that beauty can emerge from brokenness. This book is a testament to courage, grace, and the unstoppable power of a shared story.

– **Mrs. Rosena Stubbs;** *Director, Audit & Assurance, Deloitte & Touche*

ROSES IN BLOOM

Roses in Bloom

Seven Bahamian Women

Share How Resilience and Faith in God Transformed Their Dark Seasons of Divorce into Seeds that Bloomed into Purpose and Destiny!

VISIONARY AUTHOR

MICHAELLA ANN FORBES

CONTRIBUTING AUTHORS

ANISIA FERGUSON
LYNN PEGGY MCKINNEY
LISA WHITE
RAQUEL BAIN
LYNIEKA DREW
SHILAND A. BOSFIELD

Published by Purpose Pulse Publishing, a division of Purpose Pulse Management
www.PurposePulseManagement.com

Disclaimer:
This anthology contains personal stories, spiritual reflections, financial insights, and individual opinions intended solely for general inspiration and entertainment purposes. Although contributors may reference spiritual guidance, wellness practices, financial decisions, or life lessons, nothing in this book constitutes professional, legal, financial, medical, mental-health, pastoral, or therapeutic advice. Readers should seek qualified professionals for situations requiring expertise. Neither the publisher nor the contributors make any guarantees regarding the accuracy, completeness, or applicability of the material presented. Any reliance on this content is at the reader's own discretion and risk.

Each chapter represents the contributor's own memory, perspective, and interpretation of events. These accounts are subjective and may include personal beliefs, opinions, or recollections that differ from the experiences of others. Names and identifying details may have been changed or omitted to protect privacy. Any resemblance to persons living or dead is coincidental unless explicitly stated. The views expressed are those of the individual contributors and do not necessarily reflect the official position of Purpose Pulse Publishing or its affiliates. The publisher and contributors disclaim liability for any direct, indirect, incidental, or consequential damages arising from the use or interpretation of this publication.

ISBN: 978-1-971101-00-2

Contents

Foreword

There are books that inform, and then there are books that transform. Roses in Bloom belongs to the latter. It is a courageous collection of stories written by women who walked through the valley of divorce yet refused to let their valley become their identity.

Roses do not begin as bouquets. They begin as seeds hidden in dark soil. These women experienced that darkness. They were buried under betrayal, abandonment, financial strain, loneliness, and the quiet ache of rebuilding life from the inside out. Yet even in the unseen places, God was at work. Isaiah 61:3 reminds us that He gives beauty for ashes and joy for sorrow. Every chapter in this book is proof.

What makes Roses in Bloom powerful is not perfection but honesty. These stories are unfiltered and full of faith. They speak of lessons learned the hard way, obedience discovered the long way, and healing received the holy way. They show women who prayed, planned, waited, cried, trusted, and kept moving. They show that divorce may change your status, but it does not cancel your purpose.

As their pastor, I watched some of these journeys unfold. When we created a divorce recovery small group at Bahamas Harvest Church, we simply wanted to offer a place of safety. God turned it into a greenhouse for restoration. In that room, laughter returned, identity lifted, and hope took root. This book is the harvest of those seeds.

You will notice that these stories are not only spiritual but practical. They address finances, family, single parenting, wisdom, courage, and the daily disciplines required to rebuild life with dignity. Faith in these pages is not abstract. It rolls up its sleeves. It takes counsel. It makes decisions. It trusts God and still takes the next step.

You will also see the strength of community. No rose blooms alone. Every author honors the people who watered their faith and believed for their future when life felt fragile. My prayer is that this book becomes that same encouragement for someone else.

And while these pages rightfully center the voices of these women, I also want to acknowledge something important. Behind every divorce there are two stories, two histories, and two hearts that once hoped for forever. Some of the former husbands represented here also worshiped within our church family. This book is not written to vilify them, nor to paint them as one dimensional characters. Life is complicated. People are complicated. Hurt often comes from places of unresolved wounds, unhealed patterns, and unmet expectations on both sides. The God who redeems these women is the same God who desires redemption for the men as well. Grace is wide enough for every person in these stories, and restoration in God's eyes is never limited to one side of a broken marriage.

To every woman who picks up this book wondering whether anything beautiful can come from your broken season, I offer this assurance: you are not buried; you are planted. Psalm 126:5 says, "Those who plant in tears will harvest with shouts of joy." That harvest is possible for you.

To the authors, thank you for your bravery. You have taken your pain and turned it into a path for others to follow. Your stories remind us that God never wastes a wound, and He never abandons what He plants.

Step into these pages with expectation. You may come carrying ashes, but I believe you will leave carrying seeds.

- **Pastor Mario Moxey;** *Bahamas Harvest Church*

Introduction

I will never forget the moment. It was Saturday, November 8th, 2025, late at night.

The house was quiet, wrapped in the quiet stillness that only comes long after everyone else has gone to bed. The ceiling fan hummed softly above me, moving the night air in lazy circles as the glow from the screen of my laptop cast a golden hue over the room. On the screen in front of me was the final cover design of *Roses in Bloom*. The colors. The texture. The title. It was everything I had envisioned and more.

I stared at it for a long time before I realized I was smiling. My chest rose and fell in one deep, grateful breath, the kind that comes when you know you've crossed into something holy. I whispered, "Lord, I thank you" and clicked *approve*.

Just like that, it was done. But really, I knew it was only beginning.

In that quiet moment, with the soft light reflecting around me, and tears welling up in my eyes, I had an even deeper appreciation of how far God had carried me. It wasn't just a book cover I was approving, —it was a story, an assignment, a living testimony.

The years leading up to that night had been an adventure, to put it nicely! Between trying to rebuild and put together the pieces of my life after my 13-year marriage ended in divorce in 2022, and then heading from that straight into a season where the Lord guided me to leave my job and step out on my own as a business owner.

I was now learning how to build again, how to breathe again, and how to trust that broken seasons could still bloom into beauty. But on that night, November 8th, 2025, it all came together. I wasn't just remembering the woman who had survived with resilience and faith. I was meeting the woman who had finally *bloomed*.

Coincidentally, that night also marked exactly one week since I stepped fully into spirit-led entrepreneurship, leaving behind the comfort and predictability of a 9 to 5 career (and steady paycheck!) to walk by faith. For the first time in my life, I was blending every gift God had given me—the precision of planning, the structure of accounting, and the creativity of storytelling—into something that made complete sense.

My gifts and my work had become a business and a ministry. My calling had become clear. And the women I was called to serve?

They were reflections of me: builders, believers, visionaries who had known both heartbreak and hope, and were ready to turn their pain into purpose.

That night, I understood that I wasn't just publishing a book and formally launching my company. I had fully bloomed into the next level of my purpose.

When the Flowers Wilt

Only a few days before, I had an interview with Makeva Wallace, coordinator of *The Bahamas Bridal Show.* We spoke about weddings, about the business of celebration, and the beauty of beginnings. For years I had been part of that world—walking the runway, a model (literally and figuratively) to women who were dreaming of their happily ever after and their own forever.

As someone who has had her own journey through marriage, divorce, purpose and business, I naturally wanted to get Makeva's insight to include in the introduction for this book. And sure enough - that golden nugget came out in our conversation when Makeva said something that landed right in my spirit: "No one talks about what happens when the flowers wilt."

That sentence stayed with me. Because I knew exactly what wilted flowers looked like.

I knew the silence that follows when the music fades and the guests go home. I knew what it meant to smile in public while your private world quietly came apart. I knew the ache of carrying beauty on the outside while battling brokenness on the inside. And I knew the courage it took to rise again when everything that once defined you had fallen away.

That single phrase, *when the flowers wilt*, was the perfect description of the seed that bloomed into this anthology.

The Reality of Bahamian Women

When people picture The Bahamas, they see turquoise waters, pink sand beaches, and postcard-perfect smiles. But beneath that paradise exterior, real women are waging invisible battles.

We are the planners, the providers, the prayer warriors. We are the ones who stretch five dollars into five days, who lead with grace at work and intercede in prayer at home. We're the backbone of our families, the quiet strength of our communities, and the soft places where others find rest—even when we have none left for ourselves.

We balance excellence and exhaustion. We smile even when our hearts ache. We pray not only for deliverance but for discipline—to keep showing up while we wait for what God promised.

And yet, through it all, we keep becoming. That is the miracle of Bahamian womanhood: we may be pressed, but we do not break. We may bend, but we rise again with beauty and fire in our bones.

Roses in Bloom exists because our stories deserve to be seen, celebrated, and studied. The world sees our smiles. This book shows our strength.

The Garden That Grew From Grace

Every rose begins as a seed—small, unassuming, unseen. It must be buried before it can break ground.

That's what this anthology is: seven women, each carrying a seed of faith buried beneath seasons of loss, heartbreak, illness, and transformation. Seven stories rooted in God's grace. Seven testaments to the power of resilience.

Together, we became a garden—each woman representing a distinct color, fragrance, and revelation.

Lynieka, the **turquoise rose**, embodies calm strength and restoration. Her story reminds us that healing doesn't erase the past—it redeems it, turning scars into symbols of survival.

Lynn, the **pink rose**, blooms with tenderness and courage. She teaches us that true self-worth isn't found in perfection, but in the process of rediscovering who God says we are.

Lisa, the **red rose**, stands for wisdom, discipline, and quiet fire. Her journey is a reminder that faith and financial stewardship can coexist beautifully—that God honors both prayer and planning.

Shiland, the **hot pink rose**, radiates passion and renewal. Through heartbreak and illness, she rose from ashes like a phoenix, proving that purpose often emerges from pain and that joy can live again after loss.

Raquel, the **burgundy rose**, represents maturity, endurance, and grace through every season. Her story reminds us that divine timing refines us—and that real strength is gentle, not hardened.

Anisia, the **purple rose**, blooms in patience and divine expectation. Her faith in waiting—through loss, transition, and trust—shows that delay is never denial when God is the gardener.

And I, **Michaella**, the **lime green rose**, stand for renewal, growth, and divine awakening. My story is one of stewardship and surrender—proof that when you align with God's plan, your gifts, pain, and purpose all find their place.

Each of us had to be buried before we could bloom. Each of us found God in the dark and chose to grow toward the light.

In this garden of grace, **SEEDS** represent the hidden seasons—heartbreak, disappointment, waiting, stewardship, and surrender. **BLOOM** represents the revelation—the courage to grow again, believe again, and walk in purpose when everything around you once screamed defeat.

Together, these stories remind us that nothing in life is wasted—not even the pain.

The Rib Revelation

It wasn't until a week before publishing, right after the book proof was ready, that I realized: the acronym for *Roses in Bloom* is **RIB**. I paused as it hit me. Then I read it again. R.I.B.

Not the rigid, overused caricature of "the rib" that many women were taught in church, but the original image in Genesis—woman crafted with intention, formed near the heart, created with purpose. A rib is protective. A rib is foundational. A rib is essential for life.

And here we are—seven women whose marriages had ended. Women who once stood at altars believing in forever. Women who tried to build homes and hold families together with prayer, faith, and sheer endurance. Women, including me, who watched vows unravel and had to learn to rebuild from the ground up.

At first, seeing RIB in the title felt like a contradiction. But the more I sat with it, the more I realized: **our identity was never tied to being someone's rib—our identity was tied to being God's creation.**

Marriage ending does not cancel purpose. Divorce does not rewrite design. A broken covenant does not break a woman's calling. And then another layer hit me even deeper:

Every single woman in this anthology is a **mother**.
Each of us carries evidence of seed—children who bear our love, our prayers, our sacrifices, and our legacy.

Even when the marriage changed form, the seed did not.
Even when the relationship ended, the fruit remained.
Even when the story shifted, the purpose continued.

And suddenly, the title wasn't just beautiful.
It was prophetic.

Roses in Bloom. R.I.B. *Not defined by the role we once held, but by the woman we have become.*

Still essential. Still whole. Still carriers of life. Still blooming—just in a different season, a different soil, a different assignment.

We are not "former ribs." We are *Roses in Bloom*—women planted by God, flourishing under His care, blossoming in His timing. What the world may call an ending, God called a planting. And this book is the proof.

What You Can Expect from These Pages

If you came looking for pity, you won't find it here. What you'll find instead is *power.*

These stories shared by the co-authors are all unique, but they are real. They are not polished fairy tales—they are faith-filled field notes from women who survived the flood and learned to build again. You will meet women who faced divorce, illness, betrayal, loss, and financial storms—and found their way back to peace.

You will see the pattern of pain giving birth to purpose, prayer turning into progress, and resilience becoming a rhythm.

This book is not just about surviving. It's about *succeeding*—spiritually, emotionally, and even financially. Because faith doesn't dismiss practicality. These women learned to pray and plan. They learned to wait on God while working their way toward the vision. They learned the delicate balance between faith and foresight, belief and budgeting.

If you've ever cried in your car before walking into work, this book is for you. If you've ever been in the darkness unable to see a way forward but yet you still whispered, "Lord, I trust You anyway," this book is for you. If you've ever felt weary in your waiting, wondering if God forgot your name—this book is for you.

You will not just read these stories. You will feel them. And, in the end, you will find your own reflection staring back at you: the woman who is not finished yet, but already flourishing.

The Financial Faith of Bahamian Women

There's a quiet wisdom that runs through every chapter here—a theme many never speak about, but every woman lives. It's the faith that doesn't just pray for a miracle, but prepares for it.

We are a nation of women who understand the rhythm of resourcefulness. We budget in faith. We invest in wisdom. We plan for tomorrow even when today feels uncertain.

These women have lived what I call *financial faith*—the blend of stewardship and surrender. They delayed gratification. They counted the cost and paid it. They learned to put money where it could grow instead of disappear. They built not just for survival, but for legacy.

Because faith without structure is chaos, and structure without faith is empty. Together, they form the foundation for abundance.

Why You Need This Book

Because too many of us were taught to shrink when we were made to shine. Because too many women still believe that starting over means starting from nothing. Because there's someone out there who needs to know that divorce is not the end, heartbreak is not the death of destiny, and waiting is not wasting time.

This book is not just for women who have survived the storm—it's for those still standing in the rain, believing that sunlight is on the way.

Through these pages, you'll learn how to rebuild your faith, your finances, and your future. You'll see what happens when seven women say "yes" to healing, and "no" to hiding. You'll see that every thorn has a testimony.

The Gardeners Among Us

Every rose in this book tells a story of growth, but no flower blooms alone. Behind every woman's breakthrough, there was someone who watered her spirit, tended her soil, and believed she could bloom again even when she could not see it herself.

Across these pages, you'll see one truth echoed again and again—the power of mentorship and spiritual covering. Every woman in *Roses in Bloom* carries the fingerprints of those who guided her, prayed for her, and stood with her in the garden of becoming. For many of us, that guidance began within the walls of Bahamas Harvest Church, under the leadership and pastoral care of Pastor Mario and Erika Moxey.

Through the Fusion Singles-Healing after Divorce Ministry, our Pastors helped us create a safe space where broken hearts could breathe again. It was there that we met one another, women walking through endings that God was quietly turning into beginnings.

Through his teaching, compassion, and steady reminder that healing is a process, Pastor Mario helped us see that grace doesn't erase the past; it redeems it. His words, and the community he cultivated, became the soil from which these stories grew.

Beyond the pulpit, each of us was also shaped by other gardeners—our mothers and grandmothers, mentors and friends, colleagues and confidantes—those who spoke life when we wanted to give up, who challenged us to grow when comfort called louder than calling.

That's why each chapter in this anthology ends with a special dedication—a moment for every author to honor the ones who watered her spirit, pruned her perspective, and protected her purpose. These dedications are not mere acknowledgments.

They are the roots of our collective story, the evidence that we were never meant to grow alone.

Because bloom doesn't happen by accident. It happens through community. Through covering. Through the hands that help hold you up when you no longer have the strength to stand.

So as you read these stories, remember: every rose here was once a seed in someone's care. And in honoring our gardeners—especially Pastor Mario, who has sown deeply into our healing—we honor the God who brings beauty from broken ground.

Final Note From My Heart

When I hit *approve* on that final cover, I realized something. I wasn't just approving a book—I was approving a new chapter of my own life.

I was saying yes to the woman I am becoming and to the women who will come after me. I was saying yes to the process—the pruning, the pressing, and eventual bloom.

This anthology is more than ink on pages. It's a garden planted with stories, faith, and wisdom that will outlive us all.

So, to every woman reading this: whatever your season, know this—God is not finished. The soil may feel heavy now, but something beautiful is breaking through.

Celebrate every thorn that made you stronger.

Give thanks for every season that taught you to trust.

And treasure every petal that reminds you — grace still grows here.

Welcome to *Roses in Bloom.*
This is your garden, too.

For My Good

ANISIA FERGUSON

As a little girl growing up, I would sit in front of the television with my eyes glued to the screen as I watched fairytale after fairytale, I would dream about my wedding day and living happily ever after with my very own prince charming. As an adult, I now realize that these fiction stories are just as their name describes, a fiction.

Did Cinderella and the prince serve together with similar purposes? Did the prince make sure that Snow White was taken care of like the seven dwarfs did? Did Beauty continue to share her dreams with the beast after he turned into a prince? What exactly did the words "and they lived happily ever after" mean.

Marriage was nothing like I thought it would be but then again how could it be when the Holy Spirit said to me many times, "This is not the man for you". But with my strong personality and sometimes hard headedness I chased what I hoped would be my “happily ever after” based on what I saw on the screen not realizing that what I searched for already existed.

The Year Everything Shifted

The year was 2014, a year that I describe as a turning point. I was going to be 30. In my opinion and according to the standards of the world, it was time for me to be married and have children.

I was feeling the pressure of society and the man I was dating seemed to be a prime candidate for marriage. He was single and we shared the same faith. I prayed for clarity on my future spouse and God showed me clearly three times that he was not the one for me to marry.

At first the answers came as silent whispers. The third time it came as a shout, and there was no doubt in my mind that he was not the man God had for me. However, my desire to be married was so great that I knowingly chose to disobey God and ignored all His attempts to save me from what He knew would not be good for me. The bible verse “to the hungry soul every bitter thing is sweet” couldn't be more accurate in this situation.

I gave into feelings and the pressures of the world and made a covenant with a man that today I pray that my son is the opposite of and that my daughter never dates someone of his kind.

I always knew that there was a calling on my life and that God would give me a testimony and at that time I hoped it would be one of turning my marriage around, but He had a different plan. He was indeed giving me a testimony, one of restoration, resilience and one that leaves me in awe of his mercy and grace.

Resilience in the Making

The things we experience in life often shape our character, but the type of character that is formed is still dependent upon our nature. For me, I guess you can say that I have a strong temperament, a fact that has resulted in both the good and the bad in my life. But one thing that has been constant; despite the mess I make of things; God always takes it and uses it for my betterment.

I have walked in disobedience, choosing my way over His, and having to face the negative consequences that result. Yet it was in these difficult moments that I recognized my strength and resilience. Although I did not identify the overcomer spirit in me until I was an adult. In hindsight, it was birthed even in my youth.

The Beginning

Remember I said that the things we experience in life often shape our character. Well, it formed mine. As a very young child, I watched my mother as she dealt with infidelity from my father within their marriage. I vividly recall one night; she woke my brother and I up from our sleep as we embarked on a quest to find my father.

When we finally located him, he was with his mistress and a terrible argument followed as my mother confronted him. I still to this day remember the deep pain in her voice and I think that was where my resilience unknowingly started to be birthed. I was only seven years old, but I wanted to be strong for her, to be her support system and to help her through her hurt so that one day she would be okay again.

I can't honestly say that I heard the Holy Spirit's voice as a young girl when my strength born out of survival began to be cultivated, but I believe wholeheartedly now that He was in the midst. My will to keep encouraging my mom and to continue to move forward despite the turmoil we were experiencing could have only been possible with Him.

All throughout my adult years, the Holy Spirit has been a constant factor in my life, confirming every step of faith that I took, giving me strength to face trials and shaping my resilience.

There have been two major events: divorce and losing my long-term job; that were intended to destroy me, but God never left me and turned what was meant for my bad into good like He always does!

When I finally made the decision to walk away from a marriage that I was never supposed to be in and accepted that God did not want me depending on a job but fully reliant on Him; I felt His never-ending presence, and I felt His peace that surpasses all understanding.

Living with the Consequences of Disobedience

Despite my deep relationship with God, I did say that I, knowingly walked in insubordination when I chose to marry my ex-husband despite the Holy Spirit's revelation. At that time in my life, I only trusted God with certain areas of my life and I yielded to the pressures of people's opinions who saw me and my husband in our dating stage and thought that he was a good catch instead of surrendering fully to God.

There were many times in the marriage when I was plagued by that decision to walk in that rebellion. But I stayed because as we say in The Bahamas, I had made my bed and now, I had to lie in it hoping that eventually the marriage would be successful and bring God glory somehow. However, it was the opposite and very much unlike what I had dreamed about.

I eventually accepted the truth and understood that the man that I chose who had proven himself unworthy of even dating should have not been the man I committed myself to for the rest of my life. Lord, "I made a huge mistake, I am deeply sorry, and I repent".

Staying When I Should Have Let Go

It was disappointing to come to that conclusion time and time again in my marriage but nevertheless, I stayed, and I tried and eventually we were blessed with two children. While their births brought bliss to my life, there was increasingly less joy in the marriage. Our family was growing, but I was carrying the burden of providing for everyone's physical and financial needs by myself.

My husband was unemployed for most of our marriage and when he did get a job, he would only spend a couple of months there before he would get fired and be looking again. This cycle added another layer to our already fragile union and marked the beginning of the end because I could no longer handle all the weight of carrying him plus the entire family financially.

After five years together, I decided I had had enough. I made the decision to choose peace instead of turmoil, to choose uncertainty with God rather than certainty with a dead marriage and put away this selfish desire to be a wife by any means necessary.

Around that time, my relationship with God as a Father had started to evolve where I trusted Him fully as He had proven Himself to be faithful repeatedly despite me not deserving it and I realized that He always only wants what is best for me as His child.

When My Body Broke Down and My Marriage Did Too

Before the divorce, I started battling an illness that left me extremely tired daily. My husband and I were still living together at that time. One day because of an argument my husband left the marital home for nearly a month to live with his family. It was during that time that he displayed characteristics that were even worse than I expected.

He was unfaithful even though we were still married and showed no interest in caring physically for our children. I was now battling an illness which left me experiencing daily fatigue while still having to care for a three-year-old and a six-month-old on top of going to work and making sure that all our bills were paid.

It was the hardest time of my life, but it was a defining moment when my resilience kicked fully in with the grace of God. I knew that my children needed me, not only to take care of them physically, but also financially.

At less than 100% physically, I still worked two jobs to ensure I kept everything in order. I got up early every morning to get us out to school and work on time, and went to bed late, preparing for the next day to minimize any delays in the morning.

In my opinion, I believe that my husband's intentions when he left was for me to feel the stress of having to completely go through everything alone and to break me. But what he did not know was that my God was working it for my good.

His leaving when he did was not burying me but was instead fertilizing the seed planted within me those many years ago, to now spring up into a tree of resilience and strength like none other. It was the beginning of God preparing me to fully depend on Him and only Him.

Choosing Divorce and Choosing God

When I eventually decided that divorce was the best option for me, after consulting the Holy Spirit there were many persons opposed to my decision but at this point, the opinion of others did not matter. I fully trusted the message I received from the Holy Spirit that never leads me wrong that said, "It is time to let go of what I never intended for you".

When I listened to that voice, Philippians 4:7 came alive which says the peace of God, which passeth all understanding, shall keep your hearts and minds through Christ Jesus. I know that the fire of an overcomer that now burns within me, began as a spark in my childhood and the foundation is God. With Him nothing is impossible!

I am convinced of that fact without a shadow of any doubt. It is all about Him. It is by His strength, His covering, His grace, and His mercy that I went through with the divorce and came out better not bitter.

God has repeatedly shown me that He can work all things together for my good, and He is turning everything that the enemy meant for evil for my Good! I am the robust woman that I am today only because of God.

The divorce proceedings were coming to an end and eventually after some adjustments, I gained a new rhythm in my new life of being a single mom and taking care of my children and my future started to look brighter and then the unthinkable happened.

When My Security Was Shaken

At the time that I needed financial stability the most, my job of fifteen years was now in jeopardy, and I was eventually let go. When I thought I had just started to figure it out and confidently handle life on my own with my children, God had another plan to take my preparation even further. The loss of my job was heartbreaking and indeed unfair, but God reminded me immediately that the battle is not mine, but it is the Lord's.

By now, I had come to realize that it was better to do things God's way, and even though my flesh wanted to fight, I let it go. It was just one month prior to my termination that I watched a sermon by Dr. Lola Moore Johnston called "Learning to fight." In that sermon she said there are times when God would tell you "Put on your boxing gloves it's time to fight" and there are times when God would say "Be still, I got this! Those words remained with me and The Holy Spirit reminded me of them at the right time!

I recall being summoned to the office by my administrators and after that meeting I knew that I would be fired. I remember having a feeling of despair, and then the Holy Spirit whispered to me in a sweet reassuring voice "This is the way I am getting you out of here so just allow me to do it," and so that is what I did. I was going to Be Still and watch Him work.

And He did! God rewarded my submission and showed up in a mighty way. My termination was an act of love from God. This time, I was rewarded for my obedience. He worked it all out and I did not have to do anything! Yes through that process, there were still moments of fear, and sadness, but deep down I knew God was up to something big and The Holy Spirit remained with me.

I can recall the morning after I was terminated I woke up to a WhatsApp message from a friend, who at the time did not know that I was recently terminated, and in that message was a photo with the words of this bible text" "Behold I am about to do something new: Even now it is coming, do you not see it? Indeed, I will make a way in the wilderness and streams in the dessert" What assurance!!!! Sweet comfort from my Savior that He was going to take care of me and my babies, and those were the words I clung to!

Learning to Be Still and Let God Fight for Me

I could have taken the job situation into my own hands and done things the way I felt it should have been done, like I did when I chose to marry my husband, but that taught me well the consequences of disobedience.

Instead, I put my will and desires aside and prayed through the entire ordeal, allowing God to work it out as He saw fit, and I am proud of myself for seeking His will above mine. That experience was a time of significant spiritual growth for me and it truly affirmed my faith.

In the past, I would have done what I wanted to do. Now, I am allowing God to fully order my steps and lead me in the path that He desires. I also realized that I am now hearing the voice of the holy spirit with increasing clarity.

That is the most rewarding part for me that I am most proud of. That signifies that my walk with God is stronger, my relationship with Him is no longer categorized by selfishness, with me doing all the asking of Him, but I now also listen to hear His voice, thus allowing Him to ask of me, to take charge of my life.

If you are reading my story, I want to remind you that whatever we may face in this life, whether because of our disobedience or not, we can give it to God. We can watch him work. He is a God that can turn everything around for our good, but we must allow Him to. With Him, we can have peace amid any storm, a peace that surpasses all understanding.

The Way Forward

Isaiah 55:8-9 declares that the Lord's thoughts and ways are far superior to human thoughts and ways, just as the heavens are higher than the earth. Early in my adult life I failed to recognize my worth, not only as a woman who was already enough, but as a child of God. When I allow God to choose for me, I never have to settle. I chose my ex-husband in disobedience and that is the reason why I went through a divorce. I was worth so much more than giving my life to just anyone for a title.

God knows what is best for us, and we must trust that He knows what He is doing. Every choice we make, especially the choice of whom we should marry, should be one where we allow God to choose. Pray and ask Him to reveal His will, and when He does, accept it, knowing that He sees the end from the beginning, and He will never lead us astray when we allow him to do the choosing.

Called to Help Others Heal

As I move forward now, I am certain that I want to use the things I have suffered through, and the lessons I learned to help others. I see myself as a Christian motivational speaker using my testimonies to encourage others on their life's journey.

If it is God's will, my hope and dream is to open a retreat center. A place where I can host weekend retreats where anyone, from all walks of life, can come to retreat from the cares of this world, and to regroup. This is important to me, because I believe that it is God inspired.

As life continues to change, I am still seeking God to reveal to me the purpose meant for my life . I also have thoughts about a few other things I would like to do. As a result of my divorce I desire to be certified in emotional intelligence, and would like to advocate for social emotional skills to be taught to children in school, beginning at the preschool level, as I firmly believe that if I was more knowledgeable in the area of emotional intelligence I would not have put myself in the position to marry a man that I knew was wrong for me.

Doing It Alone, But Not Without God

Right now, my biggest obstacle is balancing my health challenge with having to raise my children on my own. However, it is the avenue God uses to remind me daily that I need Him, and Him alone!

I like the way my brother, a minister, says it "When Jesus is all that you have, you have all that you need! Doing it alone can be a challenge, but it is these moments and all my trials that have helped to strengthen my resilience. I now look at trials differently. I look at obstacles differently. Now, an obstacle is a means that God can use for my good.

I look forward to being in the will of God, as it is one of the best places to be and experiencing all that HE has for me in all areas of my life. I know that God's will is what is best for me and the unconditional love I used to search for, I always had from Him and inside myself! He gave me something better than happiness and I continue to welcome joy, unspeakable joy.

And we know that all things work together for good to them that love God, to them who are called according to his purpose (Romans 8:28).

I want to encourage every girl and every woman reading this to stay within the will of God. If you are in a relationship or in any situation and you know it is outside His will, repent and turn to Him. He is the way, the truth and the light!

I am passionate about spending personal time with God so I am praying for the guidance of the holy spirit on writing a book that will help other women to see the importance of spending time with God and studying His word and will encourage them to depend fully on The Lord in every area of their lives.

I also enjoy speaking and look forward to hosting Christian retreats and seminars for women and youth as I share my story with them reminding them that God will work all things together for their good, if they allow Him to.

As an educator, and a parent, I live by the motto "It is easier to build strong children than to repair broken men". Therefore emotional intelligence is a certification I am currently pursuing so that I can instill in children the importance of making wise choices and of being emotionally intelligent.

Why I'm Sharing My Story

I'm sharing my story because I know what it feels like to trust God and still wonder if He heard you.

I know what it is like to pray, fast, and obey — and still lose what you thought you needed most. To be faithful, qualified, and loyal, and still walk out of a job after fifteen years because God whispered, "I'm releasing you."

When I got terminated, I didn't cry right away. I stood there in silence, stunned as I realized what was about to happen. I had poured everything into that school — long hours, deep care, personal sacrifice — and now it was over. I knew God had already warned me. I had heard His voice clearly, "Your time here is done." But knowing it's coming doesn't make it hurt less.

Two weeks before that, my dream of homeownership was sitting on the loan officer's desk. I could see it. I could almost feel the keys in my hand. All they needed was a job letter. But I couldn't do it. I couldn't lie. God had already told me the truth of what was coming in terms of my employment ending, and I knew better than to build a dream on disobedience. So I told the agent I couldn't go forward. And I walked away from what I thought was the biggest breakthrough of my life.

That decision broke my heart — but it also broke open my faith. Because the very thing I thought God took away was what He was preparing to also replace with something better. He moved me from Nassau to Cat Island, and it was as if He'd already gone before me.

I went from paying rent to not paying a dime. The job I received paid all of my travel expenses, all of the expenses to secure a home, and continues to give me a monthly allowance as a result of the move. I was ready to spend more than $100,000 for a house I wanted, but God had other plans. What I saw as rejection was really divine redirection.

That's why I share my story — because I've learned that sometimes God's greatest blessings come disguised as loss. If God takes something from you, He has something better in store. He'll close a door you've been praying to walk through because He knows what's behind it isn't His best.

I also share my story for the woman in the waiting — the one who's tired of hearing "trust God" when trusting Him feels like the hardest thing to do. I know that season. The one where faith and fear wrestle every day.

I remember my mentor telling me, “You can’t waver, Anisia. You can’t say you trust God and then allow your mind to wander, begin to panic and doubt God’s plan for you.” It stung, but she was right. God has shown me that He’s a God of timing — not convenience. Every time I thought He was late, He was actually on schedule.

I started to notice the pattern: two weeks before the shift, two weeks before the call, two weeks before the breakthrough. Right when I was about to give up, He’d show up. He was teaching me endurance — to stay faithful in the waiting. And yet, the hardest waiting wasn’t for a job or a home. It was for love.

After my divorce, my focus was on healing, taking care of my babies, and rebuilding my life. But time passed, and loneliness crept in quietly. I longed for companionship, being cared for, and being loved, this time the right way. So when a man came along who called me beautiful, texted me all day, and made me feel wanted again — I was enjoying every minute of it! But deep down, I knew he was not who God had for me.

One night, I got into the shower, and the truth hit me so hard it felt like the water turned to tears. I remember crying so hard I could barely breathe. From the depths of my soul I cried out to God saying “God, I don’t want to be alone, I deserve to be loved ” “When will you send the one you have for me?”

And in that moment, again the Holy Spirit spoke clearly to me saying: “Hold on, You are almost there.”

And in that moment, my tears began to subside. I already knew that obedience to God is better than companionship that isn't sanctioned by Him. True devotion comes from actively listening to and obeying God's will. I now know that God was testing my devotion to Him. He wanted to see if I would trust Him with this part of my life. So I let go. I blocked the number, and told the Lord, "I'll wait for You to choose."

That night broke me — but it also birthed something in me. Because when I surrendered what I wanted most, God started preparing what I needed most. Two weeks later — the same divine rhythm again — I received the call offering me a job in Cat Island. I prayed and with the answer from God that Cat Island was the path He was taking me I accepted the offer and began preparation to move and make Cat Island my new home. And within two weeks of being there, I met a man that after much prayer, God gave me the green light to enter a relationship with. Our relationship is Not perfect, but peaceful. Not forced, but faithful.

That's why I share my story.

Because I've learned that obedience may cost you comfort now, but it will secure your blessing later. Because I know what it's like to almost miss a miracle because you were tired of waiting.

I share my story for the woman who's been faithful but frustrated — the woman who's praying, fasting, and still asking, "When will it be my turn?" For the one thinking about settling because she's weary from being single or scared to start over. I share it to remind her that God doesn't forget. His delays aren't denials — they're divine protection.

When I look back now, I can see the thread of His hand weaving through my years of heartache and heartbreak, through my termination, and through every lonely night. Like Joseph, I can truly say: "They meant it for evil, but God turned it for my good."

The coworkers who set me up. The man who gave me affection and attention but was not meant to be my next husband. The job that let me go. The house that I let slip away. Every single thing worked together for my good — and that's the testimony I carry.

So I share my story for the woman still waiting for her breakthrough, her home, her husband, her healing. To remind her that if she trusts God enough to surrender what she loves, He will restore what she lost — pressed down, shaken together, and running over. Because sometimes the road to "for my good" runs straight through "this makes no sense."

But if you can stay faithful in the confusion, obedient in the loneliness, and surrendered in the waiting — you'll watch Him turn every loss into legacy, every delay into direction, and every heartbreak into holy ground.

The Power of Mentorship

If there's one thing I've learned through every season of my life, it's that God never leaves us without guidance — He sends people, wisdom, and timely words to light the path ahead. Mentorship has been one of His greatest gifts to me. It's been the steady hand that helped me rebuild when everything else was shaking. In my darkest moments — when I questioned my purpose, my strength, and even my worth — God surrounded me with voices that spoke life into dry places.

Through sermons, devotionals, and divine connections, He used mentors to remind me that I was seen, chosen, and capable of rising again. One of those mentors is Pastor Debleaire Snell. His sermons, his 21 Days of Prayer, and his books were like anchors during seasons when I felt like I was drifting. His words reminded me that faith isn't a feeling; it's a discipline.

Through his teachings, I learned to hold steady even when I couldn't see how God was going to work it out. Those morning devotionals became more than routine — they were oxygen for my faith.

Then came Dr. Lola Moore Johnston, whose Bloom programs for women of color taught me that purpose isn't just something you stumble upon; it's something you grow into. Her guidance helped me shift from surviving to thriving — to not just find my purpose, but to be excellent in it. She helped me to believe that even as a single mother, I could still bloom — not someday, not when everything was perfect, but now, right where I was planted.

And then there's Phyllis Green — my spiritual mother, my earthly angel. She has become like a second mom to me, guiding me through this new chapter of single motherhood with grace and wisdom.

She's the one who reminds me to rest when I'm pushing too hard, to pray before I panic, and to give myself grace when I fall short. Her words often feel like God Himself whispering, "You've got this, daughter — just keep walking."

But above all these voices, there has always been one Mentor who never leaves my side — the Holy Spirit. He's the One who told me to let go when I was holding on too tightly. The One who spoke to me through tears in the shower and reminded me, "You're almost there. Don't give up now." He's the voice that doesn't just comfort — He corrects, guides, and gives peace when nothing else makes sense.

Every mentor — human and divine — has shaped me into the woman I am today. They've taught me that mentorship isn't just about advice; it's about alignment. It's about surrounding yourself with people who pull you closer to purpose, who see your potential even when you can't.

Through mentorship, I've learned that strength doesn't always roar. Sometimes it whispers through wisdom, shows up in obedience, and blooms in the quiet confidence of knowing God is still leading.

Seeds for Your Own Bloom

Every story plants something—faith, courage, or conviction—and I pray mine has planted all three. I share mine not because it's tidy or complete, but because it's still unfolding. My life is living proof that sometimes God plants us in places we never planned to go, so He can grow us in ways we never thought possible.

When I lost my job, when I walked away from a marriage that drained my peace, when I cried in the shower asking God why I had to let go again—those moments felt like endings. But they were really the beginnings. Each heartbreak, each delay, each disappointment was a seed, buried deep in the soil of His timing. I didn't see it then, but I understand it now: the waiting was never wasted.

There were seasons I didn't want to wait anymore. Waiting felt lonely, like I was the last one left standing in line while everyone else's prayers were being answered. But God had to strip away my timelines and my tiredness until the only thing I had left to hold onto was Him. That's where trust took root. That's where my faith grew muscles.

So, these are the SEEDS I want to leave with you — truths that grow even when life feels dry, if you'll water them with surrender and perseverance.

S – Surrender to God's Timing

I had to learn that surrender is not weakness; it's worship.

You have time. You don't need to rush into what God has already promised. Every time I tried to make things happen my way, I found myself heartbroken and exhausted. But when I finally let go—when I stopped trying to force doors that were never meant to open—peace replaced striving. God's plan doesn't require panic; it requires patience.

E – Embrace Your Own Journey

Comparison is a thief of joy, and it almost stole mine. I used to look at other people's timelines—the marriages, the homes, the promotions—and wonder if God had forgotten me. But I've learned that I am not in competition with anyone. Your process is personal. God writes unique love stories and healing journeys for each of us. When you stop comparing, you start celebrating. And celebration invites joy back into your story.

E – Endure the Waiting

This one is hard. Waiting can feel like walking through fog—uncertain, unseen, and sometimes unbearable. There were mornings I woke up weary, wondering how much longer. Nights I lay awake asking God, "Did I miss it? Did I wait wrong?" But even when I couldn't see Him working, He was weaving miracles in the background. Endurance isn't about never getting tired—it's about refusing to give up. The wait refines us, strengthens us, and teaches us to trust the rhythm of grace. What looks like delay is often divine preparation.

D – Discern Your Worth

For years, I tied my worth to what I could offer, who I could please, or how much I could endure. But through heartbreak and healing, I learned this: I am the prize. You are not an afterthought. You are not difficult to love. You are not running out of chances. You are the promise that someone else will be blessed to find. When you know your worth, you stop negotiating with doubt.

S – Seek God in Everything

I've made peace with the truth that I don't need to understand everything; I just need to seek God in everything.

When I invite Him into my plans, He doesn't just open doors—He rebuilds the house. When I wait for His voice instead of following my own desires, He multiplies what I thought I lost. He has never failed me, even when His timeline didn't match mine.

The Space Between the Seed and the Bloom

No one tells you how long the middle will feel. The space between the seed and the bloom can stretch on for what feels like forever. It's quiet there—too quiet sometimes. That's where weariness lives. That's where you wonder if obedience was worth it, if surrender was smart, if faith really works.

I've been there. I've cried there. I've had moments where I said, "Lord, I believe, but please help my unbelief." But what I have learned is that that space is not punishment—it's the process.

It's where God does His slow, sacred work. The kind that happens when no one is watching. The kind that forces roots to go deeper before the flower can rise higher.

In that middle space, I learned to stop trying to rush the rain. I learned that what feels buried is actually being built. God doesn't forget the seed you planted with your tears—He waters it with grace.

So if you're there now, in your own in-between, don't give up. Don't uproot what you planted in faith just because you don't see fruit yet. Keep showing up in prayer. Keep trusting His silence. Keep believing that one day, your harvest will make sense of this whole season.

Your Bloom Awaits

When the time is right, the things you've prayed for will no longer be distant dreams—they will be your daily reality. The very areas where you thought God was silent will become the loudest evidence of His goodness.

B – Believe You Have Time

You are not late. You are right on schedule. The same God who paused the storm can pause your timeline to protect your purpose. Don't panic in the pause.

L – Live in Your Lane

Stop glancing sideways at who got married first, who bought the house, or who got the promotion. Your lane has its own pace, and your lane has grace. Stay focused and faithful there.

O – Own Your Worth

You are worth waiting for, worth protecting, worth choosing. You don't have to chase what's divinely assigned to you. You are the answered prayer someone else is waiting for.

O – Obey and Overcome

When God tells you to let go—let go. When He tells you to wait—wait. Every act of obedience builds your spiritual stamina. You'll never regret obedience, even when it costs you comfort.

M – Move with Faith

Don't let fear keep you planted in old soil. Faith means movement. Walk forward, even if it's one trembling step at a time. The same God who carried you through the wilderness will carry you into promise.

I chose purple as the color of my rose in bloom because it symbolizes royalty, wisdom, and divine purpose. Purple reminds me of the strength that comes from surrender and the peace that blooms after patience.

It's the color of maturity — the hue of someone who's been pressed but not destroyed, stretched but not broken. Purple speaks of sacred waiting, of a woman who knows her worth, who trusts her God, and who blooms only when He says it's time.

So if you take nothing else from my story, take this: You are not forgotten. You are not behind. You are not unloved.

You are a daughter of the King — and your season is coming. Hold steady in the wait, for when God finally says now, the bloom will be worth every tear that watered it.

To my mother,

Frances Ferguson

You kept loving me, believing in me and standing by me through every difficulty.

Because of you, I learned that faith is a fortress and that God always rewards obedience.

In His Time

LISA WHITE

TICK . . .TICK . . .tick! That infuriating sound was everywhere, its loud echoes vibrating in my ears, my mind and my soul. It was slow, and haunting, and I wanted it to stop. I needed it to stop! - But I couldn't make it stop.

It was so frustrating!

If I could only move, then it wouldn't matter. I felt trapped. I tried to move, straining everything within me to make it happen – yet I couldn't. The Maker, He was there, His finger holding me in place. He could move me. He could help me to move—if He would—but He was just there, waiting.

Tick . . .tick . . . tick! Again! Ugh! I wanted to scream, "When, WHEN, when will You help me?!"

As if hearing my words, the hand of the hour above me calmly answered, "In His Time".

The imagery is of a broken clock, and the protagonist is the second hand desperately trying to move—to tick, but can't. It is taunted by the ticking sound of the other clocks in the room, a sound that serves as a haunting reminder of its broken state.

I was that broken clock, or more to the point, that second hand. In my youthful ignorance, I made a decision that led me into a relationship that was flawed from the start, although I chose not to recognize it. However, even after I faced the truth of my situation, I chose to stay, wanting to hold onto the semblance of a whole family—a desire born out of my childhood.

Rooted in Strength

From a young age, I was vibrant, full of light, bright, inquisitive, and unafraid to speak the truth. But at home, there were shadows of silent struggles. My mother, sweet but silenced by financial dependence, endured the bitterness of a husband whose love came with conditions. My older brother, once strong and playful, became wheelchair-bound after a motorbike accident, his body now reliant on others for the simplest tasks.

I watched, learned, and dreamt of a better life. I made a vow: "I will never be fully dependent on anyone."

Eager to escape the dysfunction that surrounded me, and believing in my dream of building a healthier life, I married young. I hoped for safety, love, and a fresh start—but what I got was a husband who controlled with kindness, paid most of the bills, and subtly clipped my wings.

He was not a new acquaintance, but an old schoolmate. We reconnected through work—he in car sales, and I in the insurance industry. He came into my office one day to buy insurance. We didn't have a prior romantic relationship, but we were old friends, so when we met that day, it was not a grand reunion, no sparks, just the acknowledgement of a familiar face amid the transaction of normal business. He became a regular customer after that, and after a while, we began talking, then eventually dating.

Red Flags I Chose to Ignore

While we were dating, I saw a man driven towards his goals, determined to be successful. Things were good; he introduced me to his family, and I found them to be very decent people. His mother was a strong, Christian woman who strove to provide a good life for her children. She and I had a great relationship. I was not a Christian at the time, and I didn't attend church frequently, but my husband did, and he invited me to go with him.

Looking back, I can't say that he was a Christian either, but in the moment, it didn't occur to me to question it. As time passed and we continued dating, I began to notice some red flags—character flaws—that I should have paid attention to, but I chose to ignore. He had a bad temper, and he was jealous. I had seen this before in my family, so I regarded it as normal and continued with the relationship.

Soon, we began discussing the possibility of starting a family. Things were going well between us, so taking the step of starting a family with him felt right, and I eventually became pregnant. We were thrilled about the prospect of having a baby of our own and were prepared to welcome our child into our own little family. Just before the baby was born, my husband was involved in a motorbike accident and broke one of his legs.

He was still in the hospital when I went into labor, so when I gave birth, we were both in the hospital. To his credit, despite his injury, he was very supportive and very present every step of the way. We were a family now. When it was time for the baby and me to be released, the three of us went home together.

My husband had his own apartment, and when we left the hospital, he wanted our daughter and me to move in with him. My parents were very old-school and did not hesitate to tell him 'No'. While I know why they didn't approve of us living together before we were married, I see it as a mistake that I didn't do so.

If I had lived with him and experienced life with him up close, I am ninety-five percent sure I would not have married him. It would have been easier to walk away from the relationship than from the marriage.

Accidents, Addiction, and a Shifting Marriage

A few months after our daughter was born, my husband had another motorbike accident. This time, his injury was more severe. He sustained a broken neck and had to wear a halo vest for three months. It is true that the things we go through either make us or break us.

I saw my husband become someone else during that ordeal. He began drinking heavily while he was in traction, drinking almost every day to ease the pain. As a result of the drinking, he became violent, and it was almost impossible to be around him once he got drunk.

That was my opportunity to get out of the relationship, but I didn't take it. Instead, I felt sorry for him. I watched my brother go through a similar situation and spiral, so I understood what he was going through and felt it was not right to leave him alone. Also, there was our daughter to consider. I didn't want to raise her alone. She was my focus. I was raised by both my parents, and I wanted the same for her, so I stayed.

When the halo vest was removed, we began planning our wedding. We were married a month after our daughter's first birthday. Sadly, though, the drinking did not stop even after the pain was gone.

His business was growing and becoming increasingly successful, which in turn brought on arrogance and narcissism. With all these factors, the marriage was marked for trouble. I remember even before our first anniversary thinking to myself, Lord, what did I get myself into?

Living on an Emotional Rollercoaster

The relationship was an emotional rollercoaster; sometimes things were good, then bad, then good again, and then back to bad. That was how it continued. Sadly, even the 'good' days were relative because they were only good in comparison to the bad. The verbal abuse was intolerable, but I mastered the art of turning a deaf ear to it. There was always a little voice encouraging me, telling me not to worry about what I was going through because God had me. That gave me an inner peace I couldn't explain.

Two years after our marriage, we had another daughter. I was still working, which was a good thing. My husband's business was doing great. He paid most of the bills including mortgages, school fees and utilities, and we agreed that I was responsible for groceries, school supplies and insurance. My salary was not substantial. It met my basic needs, and that was it, with nothing left over for any wants or luxuries, and certainly nothing left for savings or investments.

Slowly, I began to realize that I was walking the same path as my mother—a life that looked beautiful on the outside, bound on the inside.

Not My Dream

This was not my dream. I was not going to become my mother, and I didn't want my daughters' lives to be affected either. I was determined to take control of my life and be as subtle as my husband was when he was devising his plan. I smiled and played the role for him while I quietly planned. This is where God showed his face. My youngest got sick with a terrible ear infection that kept me home because I had to physically take her to the doctor for injections, because the oral meds were taking too long to take effect, which increased her chances of becoming deaf. My employer at the time was not compassionate enough to allow me to have the time off as sick leave, and asked if I preferred paying back the time with vacation or a salary deduction. Without a second thought, I said, "Take it from my vacation," and started sending out resumes. I sent my resume to companies with the hope of finding a better job with a higher salary and better benefits. I was anticipating being able to do more and possibly move on.

A Door Opens: My First Steps Toward Freedom

In less than a week, I received a job offer and accepted it, leaving the insurance company after thirteen years of working there, starting right out of high school. There is a time for every season under heaven, and the time had come for me to begin to move.

The new job was great! I felt that it was a step up to a more sure footing, and I was excited by the prospect of being in a better financial position. I invested in myself and worked hard, stashing away money, acquiring new skills, and nurturing my vision. Piece by piece, I built a life raft—not just for myself, but for my daughters. My girls would grow up knowing what independence looked like, what strength sounded like, and what love should feel like. They needed to know that there was more to life and love than what they saw in my marriage. I couldn't let them grow up thinking that settling for less was normal. Something had to change—and that something was me.

And I didn't just break the cycle—I rewrote the story.

I was determined. And soon, that determination paid off—the new job opened the door to another, with a higher salary, better benefits, more opportunities, and real room to grow. For the first time in a long time, I felt empowered. I found myself surrounded by people who didn't just talk about money—they taught me how to have it, how to manage it, and how to let it work for me.

Planning with Wisdom and Strategy

I planned my finances carefully. My investments would mature right around the time my kids were finishing high school. I told myself that if he hadn't changed by then, I would walk away. That day came, and he hadn't changed, so I did what I promised myself I would do—I left.

There has always been the nagging question of why I stayed so long in the marriage, enduring so much emotional abuse. It sometimes feels like time wasted, but in my spirit, I know that it was God who kept and guided me through it all. Ecclesiastes 3:1 says that "To everything there is a season, and a time to every purpose under heaven...." With Him, nothing we go through is wasted, neither time nor pain. I believe that because it was the right time, it allowed me to have a smooth transition out of the marriage.

The decision to leave came after twenty-two years of marriage. I became burdened by the situation, and I began struggling with the decision whether or not to leave. I believe it was God nudging me, telling me that it was time to move. At first, I wasn't sure what God wanted me to do, but as the pressure increased for me to make a decision, I sought God earnestly about what to do.

Fasting, Retreat, and a Clear Word from God

It was August 2020, during the COVID-19 epidemic. Our marriage relationship at that point was non-existent, and we were practically living like roommates. I decided to go on a solo retreat and rented an Airbnb. It was in a secluded place, and I retreated there with just my Bible, some apples, berries, and water. That was the only food I had for two days. I immersed myself in the Word and prayed constantly. I asked God to reveal to me all I needed to know, and whether or not I was making the right decision.

On the last night of my retreat, I went to bed, but was awakened by a voice that said, "Get up. Get up and pray." I sprang up from my sleep, went outside on the balcony, fell to my knees, and began praying and praising God, and weeping. My tears made a pool around me where I knelt. When I was finished, I got up and went back to sleep as if I had never awakened. I checked out of the Airbnb the next morning and went home.

After that weekend, God began revealing things to me about my husband. He reminded me of things that he had done to me, but I had forgotten, all because I just wanted my family. When he was drunk, my husband used to say, "Why don't you pack your shit and go back to your old lady dem?"

Oh, be careful little mouths what you say. Looking back, I can laugh about it now.

The separation and divorce proved to be the proverbial turning point. It awakened dreams within me that had become dormant and buried during my marriage. It also brought to full force the strength and independence that had helped to sustain me amid the turbulence of my marriage.

From Divorce to a Dream

One of those dreams was to own a home. While we were married, I often discussed my desire to invest in another piece of property or house with my husband. I asked him to help me because at the time, banks were not giving mortgages to married women without their spouse. The divorce took care of that stipulation and made the dream become a reality. Out of the bitter came the sweet.

Once separated, I had no intention of paying rent for the rest of my life, so I began to think of ways to achieve my goal of home ownership, mortgage-free, because now I considered myself too old for a mortgage.

The saying is true that a crisis brings out creativity. My parents were getting old, and it was just the two of them and my handicapped brother living in our homestead, and my dad's health and strength were slowly fading. I approached my parents with the idea of turning the house over to me so that I could move in, make upgrades, and take care of them.

It was a great plan that was beneficial to everyone...or so I thought. I had four older siblings, and my proposal was met with some opposition. In the end, my dad decided to turn the house over to both me and my older sister, and I was excited about his plan.

Seeing What I'd Never Noticed Before

It was then that I saw something I had never seen before. There was a huge space on my parents' property on which I could build a nice little cottage for me and my girls. It was amazing. It was incredible that I hadn't noticed the amount of property there was before. Of course, the space was covered with trees and rubble, but it was like God had suddenly removed the scale from my eyes.

The paperwork conveying the property to us was prepared, and I went to work on getting the space cleared. When that was completed, I was astonished! It blew my mind to think that all that space had been there all that time. Why hadn't I seen it before? That question swirled around in my head repeatedly.

It felt wonderful! I didn't know how I was going to build the cottage on my own, but I knew it was going to happen. It had to happen. That was where God stepped in...again. I thought that the investments I made in annuity policies while I was married were solely for retirement; however, I had a great agent at the insurance company, and when I spoke to her about my plans, she informed me that my investments in the policies could also be used for my project.

When she revealed to me their values, for a second time, my mind was blown! The returns on the investments allowed me to get started on building my cottage without having to go to the bank to borrow. The funds were unable to cover the entire project, but every time the money was running low, God made another way. He did so repeatedly until the cottage was completed.

There were so many people God had me cross paths with who were helpful in making that dream become a reality. People I never expected would be there showed up big time!

God Makes Everything Beautiful in It's Time

When our prayers take a long time to be answered, it is easy to go to that place of questioning God's timing. I have learned through my experiences that there is purpose, even in God's delays. Without a doubt, our characters are shaped by our experiences. They either make us or break us. Beginning from my childhood watching my parents, the things I experienced in my marriage, have all taught me resilience. I am the strong woman I am today because of it.

I am in a different place now—mentally, emotionally, and otherwise—and I want to help others through my experience. I hope that I have shown you that no matter what anyone tells you about who you are, you must know and understand who and whose you are.

Be aware of red flags. Don't ignore them; always seek God's guidance before making any decision. Be courageous, have faith, and always look to yourself to find happiness. No one else is responsible for your happiness; that comes from within.

New Fears, New Dreams

For me, my biggest fear was always not being able to support my children. That sorted itself out, however, when they became adults and were able to support themselves. Now, my biggest fear is that I will never find someone to love me the way I want to be loved, and that I will die alone.

As I look to the future, I still have some dreams I hope to fulfill. I am a great cook and two of my dreams are to operate an organic café, making nut milks, butters, and unique healthy, and not so healthy foods. I make my own nut milk now. Health is wealth.

Eventually, my café will grow into a state-of-the-art kitchen and be able to feed the less fortunate. These dreams are important to me because I believe food brings people together; it's a language everyone speaks and understands. It is so satisfying to see the reaction of people when they taste something good. That brings me joy.

In addition, I want to help women going through a rough time in their relationships and marriages, and would like to have a hotline that they can call in to for help and counseling. I want others to experience peace and joy, and to have victory in all their battles. I am feeling a quiet nudge to write more. I feel like I have a lot to say – I just don't know where to begin.

Being a part of this anthology and writing this chapter has brought a lot of things to light. I always thought I had to do it alone, not knowing about all the resources that were available to assist me in this journey.

Recently, I dissected Psalms 23. This was part of a discussion I had with a friend. He asked if I knew what each verse meant. "I never really gave it much thought," I replied. He said do it and let me know what it means to you. I did and it's amazing what can come of us when we really penetrate the word. Psalms 23 became real to me on how it's all so relatable, especially the part where it says, "my cup runneth over."

I realized that God has blessed me immensely so that I can help others. Putting pen to paper is the best form of expression I've found; I want to do more of it.

Why I Shared My Story

To be honest, I never thought of sharing my story until I was invited to become an author in this anthology. When the invitation came, I said "yes" almost instinctively — not realizing that God had already been preparing me for this moment. What

I thought would be a simple reflection on my experiences turned into a deep, healing journey.

As I began journaling, the memories started flooding back — the struggles, the planning, the counting of every dollar and every cost, both emotional and financial.

I remembered the sleepless nights of trying to make ends meet while still showing up for my children. I remembered the years of carrying a marriage that had lost its partnership, the endurance it took to hold everything together when it felt like my world was quietly unraveling.

And yet, through every season, I saw God's fingerprints. I realized He had been teaching me how to trust His timing, even when it didn't match my own.

At first, I thought my story was just about survival — but as I wrote, I saw the deeper lesson. It was about stewardship, strategy, and surrender.

It was about walking with God through practical wisdom — learning to plan, save, invest, and prepare — while also trusting Him with the parts of my life that didn't go according to plan.

I thought I was managing money, but God was managing me. He was training me in patience, endurance, and discernment.

When I began sharing pieces of my story with friends and coworkers, the response surprised me. I wasn't just talking about finances; I was talking about faith. I wasn't only describing numbers or policies; I was describing how discipline, prayer, and planning can coexist — how wisdom and worship can walk hand in hand. Over and over again, people told me, "Lisa, you need to share this. People need to hear how you did it — how you survived, how you built, how you trusted."

That's when I realized this story wasn't meant to stay in my journal. My testimony wasn't just about what I endured; it was about what others could learn through it. Whether someone takes away the importance of financial discipline, the courage to prepare in secret when no one sees you, or the faith to believe that endurance pays off — I pray there's something in my journey that plants a seed of hope in theirs.

Because here's the truth: I didn't always understand what God was doing, but now I see the pattern. Every deposit I made — in my savings, in my faith, in my perseverance — was a seed for the life I live now. I didn't know it at the time, but I was sowing for my freedom.

Sharing my story is my way of giving back what life and God have taught me. It's a reminder that you can be strategic and spiritual, disciplined and dependent on God. That sometimes, faith doesn't look like waiting quietly — it looks like building slowly, saving faithfully, and trusting fiercely.

If there's one thing I've learned, it's that God's timing rarely aligns with our timelines — but His plan always exceeds our expectations. Every delay was a setup. Every "not yet" was a divine investment. And now, as I stand in the place I once prayed for, I can say with confidence: in His time, everything makes sense.

So, I share my story not because it's perfect, but because it's proof — proof that endurance bears fruit, that planning pays off, and that faith, when coupled with wisdom, always produces a harvest.

The Power of Mentorship

Mentoring has been very instrumental in my life as it has given me a head start on success in so many ways. I gained positive feedback on how to handle situations and grow from them from people like Dr. Myles Munroe, Bishop T.D. Jakes, Eckhart Tolle, and a special friend who will remain nameless. Tolle is the author of The Power of Now, and I remember listening to that audio over and over again. It was such an on-time message, teaching me how to give my full attention to whatever the moment presents and to truly live in it.

But my mentorship journey didn't begin with authors or public figures—it started much closer to home. My father was my first real mentor. From him I learned the importance of discipline, structure, and financial order. Watching him carefully separate his money—what was for our home, what was for my mother—taught me that wisdom isn't loud; it's consistent. His example planted in me the quiet confidence that comes from planning ahead and taking responsibility for what's in your care.

Later, God placed professional mentors in my path who strengthened that foundation. In banking, I was surrounded by people who taught me to think strategically about money, risk, and opportunity. They modeled what it looked like to walk in both excellence and integrity. Even my insurance agent became a mentor of sorts. She didn't just sell me policies; she educated me on how to build a financial safety net that would one day become my lifeline. Each person, knowingly or not, poured wisdom into me that helped me to make sound, Spirit-led decisions when life got difficult.

Yet, the most powerful mentor I've ever had is the Holy Spirit. During one of the hardest seasons of my life, when my marriage was unraveling and my heart was heavy, He led me into a fast. It wasn't planned; it was prompted. Through that fast I learned how to quiet the noise, how to discern His voice, and how to find peace in stillness. That divine mentorship gave me clarity that no book or course could offer.

Around that same time, a dear friend encouraged me to read Psalm 23 not casually, but deeply. He told me to sit with it until I heard God's voice in every verse. That passage became my anchor. "The Lord is my shepherd; I shall not want." Those words taught me that mentorship isn't just about advice—it's about alignment. God used that scripture to mentor my spirit, showing me that even in lack, I would never be without what I truly needed.

Looking back, I see how every mentor fit perfectly into God's timing. From my father's practical example, to the professional guidance of colleagues, to the spiritual covering of the Holy Spirit—each one shaped me for purpose. Mentorship has never been a single conversation or relationship for me; it's been a thread of divine connection running through every chapter of my life.

Now, I see myself as both student and teacher—still learning, still growing, but also pouring back into others the lessons that once sustained me. That, to me, is the true power of mentorship: wisdom that flows full circle, lifting others while continually drawing us closer to God.

Seeds for Your Own Bloom

Every decision, every delay, and every deliverance in my life has taught me that nothing is wasted in God's timing. The lessons I've learned aren't just for me — they're seeds I pray will take root in the hearts of every woman who reads this. Whether your challenge is emotional, financial, or spiritual, you can bloom again — in His time.

These are the SEEDS I want to leave with you.

S – Surrender the Past

Don't dwell on what has happened to you. Accept what is happening now. Life doesn't move forward when you're still looking over your shoulder. Healing begins the moment you stop replaying the pain and start resting in the present. God's plan is never behind schedule — His timing is perfect, even when it feels delayed.

E – Embrace Your Truth

Never be ashamed of your past. It doesn't define you; it refines you. I was always reluctant to share my story because I worried about what people would think. I live in The Bahamas — a beautiful place, but also a small one, where stories travel faster than the truth behind them. I didn't want to embarrass anyone involved or feed the local gossip mill. But I've learned that silence serves shame, while storytelling serves healing. Now, I share boldly. Because my story may be about me, but it's for someone else.

E – Evaluate Your Commitments

Don't allow commitments — even those that once felt sacred — to keep you in a place where there is no peace. I stayed longer than I should have because of responsibility, loyalty, and love for my children. But I learned that peace is not a luxury — it's a necessity. God does not call us to live bound by what He's already released us from.

D – Don't Isolate Yourself

Talk to someone. You don't have to do this alone. Healing requires honesty — first with God, then with yourself, and finally with others. Whether it's a trusted friend, a counselor, or a community of faith, let others walk with you. It's okay to say, "I'm not okay." Strength isn't silence; it's the courage to seek support.

The space between the seed and the bloom is where most people lose hope. It's quiet. Lonely. Uncomfortable. But it's also sacred. It's where faith grows deep roots. It's where patience is tested and character is proven. That's where I learned that sometimes God hides you to heal you.

And when the time is right, He brings you into your BLOOM.

B – Believe That Time Redeems Everything

Everything you've been through has purpose. God wastes nothing — not even the seasons that seemed unfair or unclear.

L – Let Go and Let God

You can't hold on to pain and peace at the same time. Let go of resentment, regret, and control. God's way is always better, even when it's harder.

O – Own Your Story

Don't let fear of what people will say keep you silent. Small communities talk — but your healing will speak louder. When you own your truth, gossip loses its power. And someone who hears your story might finally find their freedom in it.

O – Open Your Heart to Healing

Forgive yourself. Forgive others. Healing doesn't erase your past; it transforms it into purpose. What once wounded you will one day become what you use to help someone else.

M – Move in His Time

The title of my chapter, In His Time, is not just a phrase — it's a promise. Every blessing in my life arrived right when it was meant to. From the strength to walk away, to the creativity that birthed my next chapter, everything unfolded according to His divine calendar. Trust the timing. The bloom always follows the seed.

I chose red to represent my rose in bloom because red symbolizes strength, endurance, and divine timing — the core of my story. Red is the color of life, resilience, and love that's been tested but not defeated. To me, it reflects the courage to keep showing up when everything in you wants to stop, and the quiet confidence of knowing that God's promises never miss their season.

I've learned that healthy women build healthy lives — physically, financially, and spiritually. That's the journey I'm on now: connecting healthy food with healthy women, nourishing both body and soul.

If you would like to connect with me on this journey, my contact information is in my biography.

Let's rise together — healed, whole, and blooming, in His time.

To my mother,

Dorothy Turnquest

You always see beauty in the simple things and taught me to do the same - in food, in art, and in life.

Because of you, I learned that creativity heals, nourishment restores, and joy can be found in every season.

Beauty for Ashes

LYNIEKA DREW

I HEARD MY NAME from somewhere in the distance. I opened my eyes to see my twelfth-grade homeroom teacher standing in front of the class with her arms folded and looking at me questioningly. I had been so caught up in my daydream that I had not heard a word that was said.

"I am waiting for your answer," she said firmly.

I swallowed to moisten my dried throat as I thought about how to get myself out of the situation. In the corner of my eye, I saw a hand go up. It was my McDreamy, my knight in shining armour, coming to my rescue.

"Yes," the teacher said, acknowledging him.

"I know the answer," he said.

"I am sure you do," she replied.

She seemed to consider for a moment before nodding to him to answer the question. I breathed a sigh of relief. I had been saved, again.

McDreamy was my high school sweetheart, who later became my husband. It was truly young love, and at the time, we believed that what we had was forever. I still remember the thrill of sneaking around school, passing love notes in classes, and the emotional high that a teenage romance can bring.

Is it possible that at the time I wanted so badly to believe that someone could actually love me deeply enough that nothing would ever separate us? People often say that the most important relationship a child has growing up is with their mother.

I desperately craved the love of my mother but felt deprived of it throughout my life, so when I began receiving attention from this boy in high school, I gravitated to that love and held onto it.

A Childhood Without a Safe Place

I did not have a normal childhood with parents and siblings living together in a traditional family. Instead, I was born to a young, unwed mother who struggled with substance abuse, and in addition to her youth, she was not ready to be the mother I needed. It was my grandmother who raised me while also bringing up seven children of her own.

From the time I was able to remember, my mother was hardly in my life, and when she was, my grandmother always came to my rescue. I remember hearing stories of her coming to take me out of base houses looking dirty, underprivileged, and unkempt.

I still have sporadic dreams about those days, but thankfully the innocence of youth protected me from understanding and remembering all that I was exposed to, yet I know they were not things any young child should have to endure.

Eventually, my mother met a man with whom she fell in love with and married, but for some reason, her newly formed family unit did not include me. I never really understood why I couldn't be with her.

Was it that she did not want me around, or that my grandmother would not allow me to move with her because of her lifestyle at the time?

All I knew was that I loved my mother and I very much wanted her love in return, so I pleaded with my grandmother without ceasing to be with my mom, despite her environment.

Then, when my mother began having other children, I became even more desperate to be with her, yearning to be a part of what I thought was "the perfect family".

When that did not happen, I again felt neglected and a little jealous of my younger brothers because they were able to see her all the time and I still had to live with our grandmother. I cried myself to sleep many nights because the emptiness inside me would not subside.

When Safety Shattered

Around the fourth grade, my grandmother, against what she felt in her heart was best, finally gave in and decided to let me live with my mother because it is what I desired. The house she lived in was in the ghetto, and her husband abused her physically.

There were many days when I had to call my grandmother to come and save my mother, but my mother always refused to go with her, so my grandmother took me instead. I always cried to go back, and the cycle continued until something changed.

About a year after living with my mother, my stepfather began to sexually abuse me. I told my mother what was happening, but she did nothing to defend me. It was during that time that I began to recognize what my grandmother knew all along...that living with my mother was not only not the ideal thing for me but it was not safe. It was not home.

After I told my grandmother what happened to me, I moved back to live with her, and I never again asked to return to my mother. I now felt violated, even more unloved, rejected and betrayed by my mother, and I remember making the decision at the tender age of twelve, that I would never allow any man to put his hands on me like my mother did and that I would leave any relationship where my future children felt like they were being mistreated.

I vowed to always protect them because no child should be left to feel helpless. At the time I didn't know how soon I would have children, but it was a promise I made to myself.

Loss, Questions, and a Father I Never Knew

It was also around that time (sixth grade) that I found the courage to stand up to my mother and strongly demanded that she tell me who my father was—something she chose to keep from me even though I practically begged her many times before. One time she finally heard me because shortly after I confronted her, she made a call to my paternal grandmother and told her about me.

I received heartbreaking news that shook me; my father had passed away the year before. I still dream and wonder about him, and what my life would have looked like had he been a part of it.

Would he have given me the care and the love that I so desperately longed for? Would he have shown me what to look out for and what to walk away from? And, would he have protected me from being abused?

Building My Own Fairy Tale

In 1999, my final year of high school, young love turned into a committed relationship. It felt good to be treasured and wanted. I knew my grandmother loved me, but hers was that tough kind of love—not affectionate at all—and since I never received that type of warmth from anyone, not even as a child, I still craved it in my life. I no longer felt neglected and rejected.

Life was wonderful, and with no responsibilities; however, a year later, everything changed. Just after graduation, we found out that I was pregnant. To his credit, my husband faced up to his responsibilities like a man and did not walk away. He continued to love me and was dedicated to taking care of me and our growing family.

He was a good provider who gave me everything I needed (and didn't need), and when we moved in together, he insisted that he alone would be responsible for all the household bills. "That's my responsibility," he said.

It was good to not have to worry about finances because even though I worked, my salary was less than my husband's. He told me instead to focus on just the household and our family needs such as grocery shopping, caring for our son, planning family vacations, and saving. It felt like I was living a fairy tale, and the future seemed bright.

We got married when our son was eight years old, and four years into our marriage, we decided to extend our family unit; we had our second child, creating the perfect pair. Life continued to be good and everything seemed perfect...until it wasn't.

When the Fairy Tale Ended

The change seemed to have come suddenly without any warning, or perhaps I ignored signs prior in naivety. My once loving and attentive husband became cold, distant, and dismissive, and with the change came the mistreatment and abuse: verbal, emotional, spiritual, and physical. He had always lived up to his word and taken care of all the bills of our marital home, but even that began to change.

First, he began falling behind in the payments, the mortgage in particular, and when that happened, the bank automatically deducted it from my personal account. It progressed to the point where he stopped paying the bills altogether and our electricity was disconnected with an absorbent arrears that I could not cover. He told me repeatedly to move out of his house even though when we built it together, it was always our home.

Suddenly my fairy tale life had ended, and I was living the life I had vowed not to all those years ago. It was not the way I expected things to be, and I wanted to believe the man I loved would return. I needed him to return. I stayed, prayed fervently, and fought to regain what we once had and still tried to fulfill my wifely duties sexually.

But it did not happen. Instead, I eventually realized that my husband didn't love me anymore the way he did when our love was young.

Maybe he had given too much at once, and was now burnt out with nothing left to give, nothing but leftover crumbs, and since the crumbs were better than nothing at all, I ate them, but in silence.

I felt that getting married had finally erased the stigma of me being a teenage mother with a child born out of wedlock, and I didn't want to replace that stigma with that of a divorce, so I kept it all to myself. Behind closed doors, I carried the deep wounds of abandonment and childhood trauma.

My perfect, fairytale world had burnt away, leaving behind smoldering trails of pain and emptiness. Eventually I stopped giving myself to him physically and that was when he pulled the carpet completely from under me, and, unfortunately, our children felt the negative repercussions of it. Then I remembered the promise I made to my twelve year-old self and I left.

Choosing to Speak, Choosing to Leave

For years I suffered in silence during my marriage, but my silence had its own price. It was eating away at my spirit. Slowly I became broken, and then God whispered to me a gentle command. "Tell someone."

And thank God I ultimately did. I sought out two married women who I considered to be trustworthy, and I told them about my marriage. I didn't speak to them together but separately and privately, and they each listened without judgment. They didn't rush me to decide about my husband and our marriage, nor did they tell me to leave.

These spiritual sisters did not try to influence me one way or the other but simply held my hand. They became my lifeline, reminding me that God is faithful, even when life feels like it's falling apart. They let me cry on their shoulders, but just for a little while, then they stood me up and helped me to find the strength I had forgotten I had.

The inner strength that had given me the courage to leave my mother when I realized that being with her was not a safe place where I should call home. That strength again gave me the courage to recognize that the house I once shared with my husband was no longer a home but a prison and I felt caged. One day, I made the decision on my own that I was again leaving, this time, the marriage, and that choice changed everything.

Love should never feel like silent suffering but that is what it had become for me. When I chose myself and stopped needing other people to choose me to feel valued, I reclaimed my worth. It was not an easy transition, my fairy tale existence had seen to that, and in my new single state, I didn't even know how to pay bills, but I had to learn.

And how to live, I had to learn that too, but I did. I found my footing and picked up my broken pieces. I stood up for myself for the first time, stronger and wiser, no longer the girl I used to be. I found that choosing peace was not giving up, it was growing up.

Beauty for Ashes

In the aftermath of my divorce, I developed a closer relationship with God. At first, I didn't know how I would survive and worried about my future, but as I started putting one foot in front of the other and listened to God's voice, I realized that I was not on my own but my Godly father was carrying me.

When all I had were broken pieces, even in the darkest valleys, God met me there and never left. He didn't just glue me back together, He reshaped me and molded me into a vessel of purpose and grace, and I discovered a deeper strength I didn't know I had, and I realized that real strength isn't developed in comfort, but through hardship.

Through my pain, I found that God is not only a healer, but He's also the ultimate provider and partner. He filled every void in my life, and He affirmed me when the silence was deafening. He showed me how to stand tall in rooms I once thought I could not enter without a man beside me, and He helped me to find my voice.

He became my mother, my father, my husband, my friend—my everything. Circumstances that happened in my life may have been the enemy's plan to destroy me, but God used them to build me. My story is living proof that with God brokenness can become beauty. He promised me beauty for my ashes, and I see it every day.

Becoming Unbroken

Today, I stand as a woman restored and still becoming. I'm a single mother of two children—an older son, my "Sonshine" and a teenage daughter, my "Mini Me"—with the love, presence, and protection I once begged for as a child. Our home isn't perfect, but it is peaceful. It is safe. It is ours.

Walking away from my marriage meant walking straight into uncertainty. For years, I had lived a life where the bills were handled and the routine was predictable, even when my heart was quietly breaking.

When it ended, I had to start from scratch. I didn't know how to manage everything on my own—but I was determined to learn. I was determined for my son, who first taught me what unconditional love looked like. For my daughter, who reminds me daily that generational healing is possible. For the twelve-year-old girl inside me who promised that no child under her care would ever feel unprotected, unseen, or unheard.

So I rebuilt—emotionally, spiritually, and financially. I kept my full-time job in banking and let God teach me how to steward my resources with wisdom. I began to see that healing wasn't only about my emotions; it was also about my systems, my structure, and my stewardship. I stopped letting fear dictate my finances and started asking, "What's already in my hand?"

For years, I had viewed entrepreneurship as survival. Now I see it as strategy. I learned to budget from a place of peace instead of panic. I learned to create margin where there used to be lack. I learned that relying on one source—whether a man or a single paycheck—was too fragile a foundation for the kind of future God was calling me to build.

My healing became holistic. It wasn't just prayer—it was planning. It wasn't just faith—it was follow-through. Today, I am still healing, still growing, still trusting. Some days I am cautious; other days, unstoppable. The lioness within me has awakened, and she guards her peace fiercely.

When I look back, I see clearly how my grandmother's grit shaped my backbone, my mother's absence deepened my empathy, and my God anchored it all in grace. I am not merely surviving my story—I am stewarding it. What once buried me has become the soil that keeps me grounded.

Living the Assignment: Streams, Stewardship, and Sisters

I no longer see my life as broken pieces but as carefully planted seeds. I still work in banking—a field that keeps me sharp and observant—but God has also multiplied my capacity. I've built additional income streams, each tied to something I naturally love and already do well. What once looked like "side hustles" are now divine strategies that sustain my family, sharpen my discipline, and serve other women.

BANKING CAREER – MY TRAINING GROUND

My 9–5 has been a classroom in stewardship. Every day, I witness how people handle money—sometimes wisely, sometimes recklessly—and I've learned that structure is as spiritual as prayer. It has shaped how I lead my home and how I now guide other women toward financial wisdom.

Cleaning Supplies & Personal Shopping Business – My Legacy Stream

This venture began as a way to supplement my income, but I soon realized that helping women maintain their homes with excellence is its own form of ministry. Providing products that keep homes fresh, organized, and cared for reminds me that excellence itself is worship.

Baking – My Heart Stream

Baking started as therapy—a creative release that filled my house with sweet aroma and warmth. Over time, it became a business that fills others' homes with comfort. Every treat I deliver represents both joy and provision; it's God turning flour and faith into financial stability.

Administrative Services and Event Planning – My Mind Stream

I've always had a gift for organization and presentation. Transforming that skill into a paid service taught me that order can also create overflow. Helping others find clarity and polish in their work became another steady stream of income—and another avenue of impact.

Each stream represents not just survival but strategy. They are the legs that hold up the table God is building for my children and me. Together, they've allowed me to stabilize our finances, rebuild confidence, and model resilience for other women learning how to stand again.

I teach my children what I'm still learning: That when you use money wisely, it is a tool, not a trap. That work is holy when done with purpose. That what's in your hand is often enough to start. These businesses didn't just fund my bills—they've funded my becoming.

And through them, I discovered something powerful: the women who buy from me, book me, or talk to me are the same women God has called me to serve. They're balancing children, jobs, responsibilities, and faith—just like I was.

When I deliver detergent, a proposal or a dessert, I'm not just completing a transaction; I'm stepping into an opportunity to uplift, encourage, and remind another woman that she's not alone. This revelation birthed my movement and brand, Unbroken: Beauty for Ashes.

It's not a business slogan—it's a mission. It's my way of creating safe spaces where women can breathe again, talk honestly, and learn to use what's already in their hands to build stability and joy. Through Unbroken: Beauty for Ashes, I see:

- Gatherings, retreats, and small groups where women can heal and rebuild;
- Mentorship programs that teach financial and emotional stewardship;

- Sisterhood circles that show how faith and strategy coexist; and
- Resources equipping single mothers and working women to build multiple streams without losing themselves

I'm not building this brand for applause; I'm building for fruit. This is my obedience. This is my offering. I'm proof that even after everything falls apart, you can rebuild—brick by brick, stream by stream, prayer by prayer—and still stand unbroken.

Why I Shared My Story

I remember sitting many nights in silence, eyes swollen, pillow soaked, wondering how my life had drifted so far from what I dreamed. I had prayed for love, but what I was living felt more like war. It wasn't just the arguments or the emptiness — it was the slow erosion of who I was. I had become a shell of a woman, showing up, doing my best, but quietly breaking on the inside.

All I could think about was survival — how to keep a roof over our head, how to keep my children stable, how to keep my faith alive. And in those quiet hours, when the house was still and my heart was loud, I told myself, surely I can't be the only one. Surely, there had to be another woman lying in bed next to someone and still feeling utterly alone.

The song "Stranger in My House" by Tamia used to haunt me because it described exactly what I was living — looking at a familiar face that now felt foreign, loving a person who no longer saw me.

There was one night I made myself a promise: if I ever found my way out, I would go back for her. The woman sitting in the dark, whispering to herself, “Is this really what life should be like”? The one smiling through Sunday service while dying on the inside. The one paying bills, raising children, keeping appearances — and slowly disappearing in the process.

This is my why. Because silence nearly destroyed me. Because pretending nearly killed me. Because keeping it together for everyone else almost cost me me.

In our culture, we’re taught to protect the image, even if it costs us our peace. We wear our pain like perfume — smile through it, worship through it, work through it — but never talk about it. I realized that’s why so many women stay stuck. Healing can’t grow in hiding. It needs light. It needs truth.

So I decided to break the silence. And when I did, I found power.

Sharing my story wasn’t easy — but it was necessary. Because every time I opened my mouth, another woman exhaled. Another woman said, me too. Another woman realized she wasn’t crazy, or weak, or faithless — she was just human.

But I didn’t stop there. I didn’t just want to tell my story — I wanted to live differently because of it.

When I walked away from what broke me, I didn’t just rebuild emotionally. I rebuilt financially, spiritually, and mentally. I learned how to make what I had work for me. Baking, selling cleaning supplies, providing administrative support — they weren't random hustles. They were streams of restoration. Every order, every invoice, every transaction reminded me that I could still stand on my own two feet.

God taught me stewardship in the storm. He showed me that the miracle wasn't just leaving — it was learning. Learning to trust His plan, learning to multiply what I had, learning to see my value in more than what someone else could give me.

That's why I tell my story. Because another woman needs to know she can pray and plan. She can have faith and still set boundaries. She can cry at night and still get up and run her business in the morning.

I didn't find the woman I needed back then — so I became her. And in becoming her, I bloomed. I'm not perfect. I'm not finished. But I'm free — and that's a story worth telling.

The Power of Mentorship

Mentorship changed the way I healed. When I couldn't pray for myself, someone prayed for me. When I couldn't see my worth, someone reminded me who I was. A mentor doesn't always have the answers; sometimes she just shows up and stands with you until you remember how to stand on your own.

It's hard to be married and feel single. Hard to sleep beside someone but still feel unseen. That's why mentorship matters. It steadies you. It reminds you that you're still loved, still chosen, still called and still seen.

It gives you perspective when emotion clouds your view, encouragement when hope feels far, and a reason to keep going when it seems so easy to give up.

We all need someone to say, "I've been there, and you're going to make it." Truth is, sometimes that's all it takes — one voice of faith in the middle of the storm.

Seeds for Your Own Bloom

Every story plants something — hope, strength, or faith — and I pray mine has planted all three. I don't share my journey to rehearse what I survived; I share it so you can see that what was buried in pain can still rise in purpose.

These are the SEEDS I want to leave with you — truths that will take root if you water them with faith, courage, and consistency.

S – Surrender

You don't have to have all the answers. Healing begins the moment you stop trying to fix everything alone and let God lead the process.

The surrender that once felt like defeat will become the doorway to peace.

E – Endure

Some seasons are hard because they are pruning you. When progress feels slow, remind yourself — a seed doesn't bloom overnight.

The ground may feel dark and heavy, but what's happening beneath the surface is divine construction. Keep showing up.

E – Embrace Empowerment

Your story still carries power, even if it began in pain. God never wastes a wound. Every scar is a testimony that reminds others it's possible to heal, rebuild, and rise again.

D – Discipline

Stay grounded. Save when it's hard. Pray when you're tired. Keep building even when no one notices. Discipline turns inspiration into transformation — it's the proof that you're serious about what you prayed for.

S – Stewardship

Take care of what's in your hands — your gifts, your peace, your story. Stewardship is how you prepare for the blessings you've been praying for. Use what you already have with excellence; God multiplies what you manage well.

The Space Between the Seed and the Bloom

This is where most people give up — the middle. The place between what you planted and what you're praying for. It's quiet here. Lonely sometimes. Uncomfortable often. But necessary.

In this space, God teaches you how to carry what you've been asking Him to create. He pulls up shallow roots, strengthens your core, and tests your endurance. You'll question if it's working. You'll want to dig up what you planted just to see if it's growing. Don't.

Trust the soil. Trust the silence. Trust the slow work of God. This is where transformation happens — not when everyone can see you bloom, but when no one sees you becoming.

Stay faithful in the middle. Protect your seed from doubt. Water it with prayer. Guard it with gratitude. The process is long because the harvest is lasting. And when the time is right... you BLOOM.

B – Believe You're Not Alone

You're not the only one walking this road. There's a sisterhood of survivors who've been buried too — and they're cheering for your rise.

L – Look for God

He's not just at the finish line. He's with you in the process — in the quiet, in the waiting, in the days that don't make sense.

When you can see His hand in the hidden places, you'll never fear the unknown again.

O – Open Your Heart to Restoration

Don't stay attached to what broke you. Let go so God can rebuild.

Your latter days will not only be greater — they'll carry the wisdom of everything that came before.

O – Own Your Strength

You didn't just survive; you evolved.

Every time you refused to quit, heaven recorded it. Own your growth. Stand tall in what it cost you to still believe.

M – Move Forward in Faith

Don't stay buried where God once planted you. Rise, rebuild, and step into what He's prepared. Faith isn't just belief — it's movement. Take what you've learned, plant it in your next season, and watch new life unfold.

I chose turquoise to represent my rose in bloom because it embodies calm strength and spiritual renewal. Turquoise reminds me of the balance between faith and flow—how peace and perseverance can coexist. It's the color of healing waters, of divine clarity, of standing firm even when everything around you shifts.

To me, turquoise is both tranquil and triumphant—a reminder that true beauty begins when we trust God enough to be still and let Him restore us.

This color has become more than my symbol; it's my testimony. It reminds me that healing doesn't mean returning to who I was—it means becoming who I was always meant to be. And as I continue to walk in my own restoration, I carry this truth: what God does in you, He intends to do through you.

That's the real purpose of the bloom—to release seed. You are the next garden God wants to grow.

The advice I shared with you, that I learned from my experiences in life, aren't just lessons — they're living seeds of survival and strength, waiting to bloom in you.

So plant them. Water them. Protect them. Believe again. Because no matter what you have gone through or may be still walking through, your story isn't over — it's just beginning to bud.

To my grammy,

Ruth Naiomi Ferguson - Saunders

You tried to shield me from every harm and taught me that love can be both tender and strong.

Because of you, strength, wisdom, and love took root and now they bloom in me.

Fearfully and Wonderfully Made

LYNN PEGGY MCKINNEY

IMAGINE A WORLD WHERE women, no matter their status, completely embrace their worth–where they rise with confidence believing and knowing that they are fearfully and wonderfully made. A world where they define themselves not by circumstances but by their boundless potential. A future where faith in their abilities overpowers outside judgment, turning every challenge into a launchpad for success. This is the world I envision.

From a young age, I was captivated by the "why" behind everything. I was the curious child, the one who peppered my parents with endless questions, seeking clarity and understanding. Thankfully, my father saw my curiosity not as defiance but as a gift. He nurtured it, cultivating the insight that now shapes how I approach life.

Confidence on the Outside, Questions on the Inside

Through my teenage years, I displayed an outgoing spirit and full confidence but there were times I felt a quiet longing to be truly seen and understood; an unspoken desire for acceptance that fueled my need to excel and to be perfect. Growing up in a home with a mother who was deeply caring and attentive, I learned the value of love and the importance of striving to do my best.

As a middle child, I often looked to her for approval, hoping my efforts would earn her recognition. Over time, I began to realize that my sense of worth became tied to meeting her high expectations, and I struggled to see my own value apart from her approval.

Then life presented unexpected challenges. An unplanned pregnancy that revealed deep wounds beneath my outward confidence. That experience brought pain and exposed a struggle with self-esteem I had not fully acknowledged–reminding me that the outward strength I often showed was sometimes a mask covering deeper feelings of insecurity.

These days, my purpose is to walk with others as they confront the hard questions of their own journeys. I thrive on this skill. Analyzing problems, brainstorming ideas, and uncovering opportunities are my passion. For me, it is like solving a puzzle where every piece has the potential to unlock something extraordinary.

When Life Unraveled

Life has a way of shaking our foundation when we least expect it. My divorce was one of those defining moments—a painful, unexpecting turning point that forced me to confront the parts of myself I had long neglected.

What began as a season of deep loss eventually became the soil for growth and transformation. From the ashes of that broken union, I uncovered resilience, rediscovered my self-worth, and found an identity anchored in God's unwavering love.

No one stands at the altar imagining their marriage will one day end. Divorce carries its own kind of grief–a mourning not just for what was, but for what could have been. It is a cycle of denial, sadness, anger and self-blame.

For a long time, I bore the crushing weight of believing I alone had failed. But through counseling, prayer, and honest reflection, I began to see more clearly. I accepted my part, released the rest, and allowed God to begin the healing work within me.

Breaking to Build Again

As a divorced mother, life demanded more of me than I ever imagined. Balancing a career, raising my children, and building a better future stretched every part of who I was. Yet, when I released the need for perfection, the phrase "a spirit of excellence" became my guiding light. It was not about doing everything right–it was about doing everything with purpose and love. Though the journey was difficult, it shaped me into the woman I am today.

There came a day when I stood in front of the mirror and whispered, "Who am I now?" The title of "wife" was gone, but the woman remained—scarred, yet still standing. Divorce can make you feel defined by failure, but mirrors only show reflections, not the full story.

With encouragement from friends, family, and coworkers, I sought counseling–a decision that became a lifeline. In those sessions, I learned to face emotions I had long buried and to separate guilt from truth.

My counselors helped me see that a healthy marriage requires two whole individuals, not one person carrying the weight for both. I also realized that my worth could not depend on another's approval–it had to be rooted in God and the strength within me.

God Close to the Brokenhearted

The end of my marriage broke me in ways I never expected. The shame, and silence were suffocating, but Psalm 34:18 reminded me, "The Lord is close to the brokenhearted and saves those who are crushed in spirit." That verse became my anchor, a promise that God was still near, even in the ruins.

Writing became my form of release. Journaling prayers, reflections, and raw emotions allowed me to process pain and witness my own progress. Looking back at those pages now, I see a journey of resilience, faith, and quiet transformation.

Learning to Stand on My Own

Financially, the road was just as challenging. Life after divorce required discipline and careful planning. Budgets became my compass, guiding me through unfamiliar territory. What began as survival evolved into empowerment—a steady reminder that I could chart my own course, no matter how rough the waters.

Most of all, I came to understand that healing was not just for me—it was for my children. They had weathered the storm too, and I was determined to create a home where they could flourish despite the pain. Parenting after divorce became my sacred mission, a season that deepened my faith and revealed God's sustaining grace.

To rebuild stability, I began creating new family traditions and rituals, inspired by the example set by my grandmother. Growing up, I had the privilege to have my father, my mother and my maternal grandmother's care. My grandmother's steady presence was our family's heartbeat.

Every morning my grandmother bathed my siblings and me, and each evening she tucked us in, asking "Who made you?" and "Who redeemed you?"--simple questions that planted seeds of faith and identity. She left her home on Cat Island to help raise us in Nassau, embodying selflessness and strength.

My grandmother's quiet heroism taught me that love's power lies in consistency and devotion. So, whether through shared prayer time, summer adventures, birthday celebrations or a simple Sunday afternoon drive, I sought to give my children the same sense of security she gave me. And when I see them now–grown, reminiscing about their childhood with gratitude–I am reminded that from brokenness can come beauty, and from rebuilding can come legacy.

Parenting with Purpose

After my divorce, my greatest fear was failing my children. Raising three sons without their father in the home often felt like an uphill climb. I wondered how I could guide them, shape their character, and help them grow into strong, compassionate men.

Those questions lingered, but instead of allowing fear to cripple me, I chose to let it motivate me. My mission became clear–to equip my sons with the values, confidence, and life skills they would need to thrive, no matter the obstacles ahead.

To keep them focused and inspired, I surrounded my sons with opportunities for growth and discovery. From music lessons, Boys Clubs such as Scouts, Boys Brigade and Men of Valour to AWANA, basketball, and softball, each experience became a stepping stone in their personal development.

I watched with pride as they gained confidence, discipline, and resilience–qualities that would serve them well beyond childhood.

Those years reminded me that parenting is not about perfection; it is about presence, guidance, and creating an environment where children can unfold into the people God designed them to be.

Facing Fear and Finding Fuel

Through this journey of parenting, I learned a powerful lesson: fear loses its grip when met with action. By pouring my energy into my children's development, I turned my worries into opportunities for them to flourish. The result was not just their growth—it was mine too. Together, we discovered that even in the aftermath of loss, life could be filled with hope, purpose, and love.

In the wake of my divorce, the journey or parenting became both my greatest challenge and my greatest teacher. It revealed not just resilience, but a deeper sense of purpose and hidden strengths I did not know I possessed. The process of healing led me to embrace the full spectrum of who I am; a woman who thrives on creativity, logic, and the joy of discovering new solutions.

Over the years, I have developed a variety of skills that balance logic and creativity. One of my favorite experiences was taking ceramics classes–they offered both structure and creative freedom, which helped me slow down, stay present, and release emotional tension. I later shared this passion with my sons.

Today, I proudly display our handmade pieces around the house. I derive joy from the act of creation. As a thinker who is both imaginative and analytical, I continually pursue new solutions to problems. Life's tapestry of challenges has taught me to stretch beyond my comfort zone. I love approaching things with a creative mindset , blending practicality with new ideas to uncover meaningful solutions.

Purpose at Work, Not Just a Paycheck

This personal transformation began to influence every part of my life–including my profession. What began as a career of policies and paperwork evolved into a platform for purpose. Each client represented a story, a family, and a set of dreams to protect.

I discovered that my ability to listen and empathize was just as vital as my technical knowledge. In many ways, the workplace became a classroom where God refined my character, teaching me to lead with integrity, patience, and grace.

My passions, however, are what truly breathe life into my days. I love listening to different music genres, transforming old materials into something valuable, and immersing myself in a good book. Reading allows me to step into different worlds, gain new perspectives, and find quiet moments of inspiration.

Creativity in all its forms–whether through crafting, repurposing, or reflection–feeds my spirit. And at the end of a long day, I still cherish the simple joy of a lighthearted sitcom that helps me unwind and smile.

Legacy for My Loved Ones

At the core of everything I do is my family. My greatest desire is to create a legacy for my sons—a foundation of love, resilience, and inspiration that will endure long after I am gone. One day, I hope to turn my passions into purpose by becoming my own boss, blending creativity with service to make a meaningful impact.

As I rebuilt my life and learned to balance the roles of mother, professional, and individual, I came to see fear differently. It was not something to avoid but something to understand and harness. Fear, when examined closely, often reveals what we value most and what drives us forward. This realization allowed me to embrace fear not as a barrier, but as fuel for growth.

After my divorce, I quickly recognized the need for strategic planning in my life. I had to be present for my children while excelling in my career. As the sole breadwinner, complacency was not an option. My children depended on me, and that responsibility became the engine that fueled my drive to work harder and rise through the ranks.

Starting in an entry-level position, I fought my way up to a senior role, refining leadership skills along the way. The challenges of balancing motherhood and a demanding career taught me resilience, time management, and the value of perseverance.

With each new season of life, fear revealed itself in different ways–shifting in form but always pushing me to grow. In this “empty nest” chapter of my life, I find myself missing the daily presence of my sons—the laughter, the conversations, the feeling of a full house.

Though I am endlessly proud of their independence and the paths they have carved for themselves, the silence that now fills the space they once occupied is palpable. I thrive on connection, and I have learned to fill that void by giving back to my community. Serving others fills me with purpose and reminds me that, even when my nest feels empty, my heart remains full.

As retirement looms on the horizon, I face the mixed emotions of anticipation and trepidation. The thought of stepping into this new stage, with all its possibilities and uncertainties, is both exciting and intimidating.

I have begun preparing by mapping out my vision for the future. My vision board serves as a constant reminder of the dreams I still want to pursue, keeping me grounded and hopeful as I look toward the future with both excitement and a healthy dose of caution.

Have I Reached My Full Potential?

Despite the many milestones I have reached and the success I have witnessed in those I have mentored, I sometimes find myself wrestling with the fear that I have not yet reached my full potential. This fear pushes me, urging me to keep striving and growing. It reminds me that failure is not the end—it is simply a step in the process, a necessary part of breaking through my own limitations and moving closer to the woman I am still becoming.

The tenderest of my fears lies in the world my granddaughters are growing up in. With the omnipresence of social media and the often unrealistic standards it promotes, I worry about how these pressures might affect their sense of self-worth.

My hope is to be a guiding light in their lives—someone who offers encouragement, wisdom, and love. I want them to know their value is not defined by likes or filters, but by the unconditional love of God. They are fearfully and wonderfully made, flaws and all.

Though these fears weigh heavily on my heart, they do not paralyze me. Instead, they inspire me to connect more deeply with others, to plan intentionally for the future, and to pour wisdom and love into my family. Fear, when acknowledged and faced head-on, does not signal the end of the journey. Rather, it serves as a reminder of what truly matters, fueling my drive to move forward with purpose and passion, no matter the uncertainties that lie ahead.

Faith, Finances, and Forward Motion

In the midst of rebuilding my life after, I discovered that faith became my steady anchor. Psalm 139:14 shone like a light in the darkness: "I praise You because I am fearfully and wonderfully made; Your works are wonderful, I know that full well." These words reminded me that my worth was not defined by what I had lost, but by who I was in God's eyes—deeply loved, valuable, and capable of beginning again..

With this renewed perspective, I turned my focus toward practical steps that would bring stability to my family. One of my proudest milestones was becoming a homeowner—something that once felt impossible. Watching a coworker, who was also a single mother, purchase her own home inspired me to believe that I could do it too. Her perseverance lit a spark in me.

When I finally qualified for my home on my own, it represented far more than financial success–it was a declaration of strength, perseverance, and faith in action. It proved that with hard work and belief in God's guidance, even the most distant dreams could become reality.

Over time, I began to understand the truth behind David's words, "It was good for me to be afflicted." At first, I could not fathom how something as painful as divorce could possibly be "good." Yet, through the struggle, I uncovered resilience and courage I did not know I possessed. The pain became a teacher, revealing hidden strengths and shaping me into the woman I was meant to be.

Divorce was not my ending–it was my transformation. Healing, I learned, was not about finding fault but about finding growth.

Through this journey, I gained compassion, maturity, and an enduring sense of self-worth. Today, I can stand with confidence and say, "I know who I am."

Humility also became one of my greatest teachers. Acknowledging that I could not do everything on my own opened the door for God to move. It was in those moments of vulnerability that I discovered the beauty of transparency and the strength in authenticity. God showed me that He cares about every area of our lives, no matter how big or small. He surrounded me with people who offered encouragement, guidance, and love just when I needed it most.

Perhaps the most challenging lesson was learning to accept what I could not change. No one begins a marriage expecting it to fail, and the grief that follows can feel like mourning a dream that died. But I came to realize that acceptance is not about surrender—it is about release. Divorce is not the end of the road; it is an unexpected detour that invites you to rediscover yourself and redefine your life. Acceptance helped me see the hidden blessings within the pain—an opportunity to rebuild, reimagine, and reclaim my purpose.

Wholeness, I discovered, is not the absence of pain but the ability to rise from it. The phrase "nothing broken, nothing missing" took on new meaning for me. It was not about achieving perfection–it was about restoration. Each step forward was a reminder that God's plan was still unfolding, and I was still becoming the woman He designed me to be.

To anyone walking through the valley of divorce, know this: you are not alone, and this is not your final chapter. Though the journey may be painful, it is also sacred. It is where healing begins, where strength is forged, and where faith deepens. Lean on your loved ones, hold fast to hope, and remember that God walks with you every step of the way. From brokenness comes beauty, and from the ashes, new life will rise.

My path as a single mother navigating heartache, faith, and personal growth has taught me profound lessons about resilience and grace. Even in the most uncertain times, I found that growth was still possible.

Today, I stand as living proof that with determination, faith, and the support of others, we can rise from our hardest seasons and step boldly into a future filled with purpose. If you are on this journey, take heart–your best chapters are yet to come.

Grace After the Breaking

As I began piecing my life back together, I came to understand a powerful truth–we are not defined by the relationships that did not last. Divorce is not a symbol of failure, but rather a single chapter in a much larger, unfolding story. Women are layered and resilient, capable of reinventing ourselves in ways we often underestimate. The true challenge lies in rewriting the story–discovering who we are beyond the titles, roles and expectations that once shaped our identity.

A major part of that rediscovery came through reconnecting with myself. I realized that self-care was not optional—it was necessary. It was not about indulgence; it was about healing. My journey back to wholeness began with small, intentional acts: returning to old hobbies, rekindling forgotten passions, and daring to dream again.

I found peace in simple things–quiet walks, moments of reflections, and the joy of a paintbrush in my hand. Each act of creativity and stillness reminded me that I was still alive, still valuable, and still whole.

Co-parenting brought its own set of tests. Yet, I made a conscious decision to put my children's emotional well-being first. No matter what tension existed between their father and me, I understood that my sons needed him to develop a strong sense of identity.

Supporting his role in their lives was not a surrender of my principles–it was a reflection of them. By focusing on our shared purpose of raising confident, grounded young men, I learned that cooperation, not conflict, would help them thrive.

In the years after my divorce, I am thankful to realize that I never walked that journey alone. My circle of support became a lifeline–family, friends, mentors, and women who had walked the same path before me. Their encouragement and wisdom carried me through some of my darkest days. Together, we built a safe space where honesty, laughter, and faith created room for healing. In that community, restoration was not just a hope–it became reality.

Rebuilding also meant learning to manage my finances with new discipline. Life after divorce required planning, budgeting, and intentional stewardship. At first, it was daunting, but I came to see budgeting not as restriction, but empowerment. Living within my means while still enjoying life taught me that financial strength was not about how much I had–it was about how wisely I used what I had been given.

Fear often tried to whisper doubt–especially when I made the difficult decision to change jobs. Leaving behind comfort and familiarity was terrifying, but I knew growth demanded courage. Questions raced through my mind: Would I succeed? Could I handle the change? But in taking that leap, I realized that fear is not a sign to stop–it is a signal to stretch.

The transition reminded me that growth rarely feels safe, but it always leads to strength. By trusting God and stepping out in faith, I discovered new purpose both in my career and in my heart.

Looking back, I can see that fear itself became a teacher. It pushed me to lean into faith, to persevere when things felt uncertain, and to believe that God's plan was unfolding even when I could not see the full picture. Each challenge–whether in parenting, finances, or personal growth–became an opportunity to rise stronger and wiser. Today, I stand proud of the life I have built, grateful for every lesson the journey has taught me.

Divorce, I now know, was not the end–it was the beginning. It was the pruning that made room for new growth, the storm that cleared the skies for light to shine through. My story is not defined by loss but by renewal. I no longer see myself as "divorced" or "single." The most meaningful title I have reclaimed is simply me.

Fearfully & Wonderfully Made: My Blueprint for Unshakeable Self-Worth

Psalm 139: 14, "Your works are wonderful; I know that full well" is one of my favorite scriptures. I am finally confident that God made me in His image and likeness and sees me as His masterpiece. No matter what I face, He will walk beside me and when I cannot walk, He will carry me. I will praise His name forever!

Through all of the ups and downs, The Holy Spirit has revealed to me my purpose in life which is to mentor girls and women who may struggle with self-worth like I did so I am so excited about the next chapter in my life where I will launch my business called "Fearlessly Female" which will help girls and women learn about wealth while expressing themselves creatively.

With a background in insurance, I serve as a consultant for women in order to build a balanced insurance portfolio that is right for them offering wealth benefits while they are living plus for the next generation. I am also working on the creative side of the business where with the first two offerings being a coloring book and crafts that will encourage girls and women of all shapes and sizes to remember that they are fearfully and wonderfully made and hold on to all of God's promises for them.

Coloring and building something unique have always been therapeutic and relaxing for me while allowing me to re-discover me and I hope it does that same for others. If you desire to connect with me, please see my biography for more information. I would love to hear from you.

My brand's deepest roots are planted in the powerful truth of Psalm 139:14: "I praise you, for I am fearfully and wonderfully made." This is not just a Bible verse; it is the blueprint for my inherent, unshakable self-worth.

Our value is a gift from God, stamped upon us at creation, and is therefore untouchable. It is the Anchor of Faith for every woman seeking true self-worth.

I know the pain of believing the opposite of my brand's promise. I saw myself as a total failure after my marriage ended, convinced I had no self-worth left. This conviction was compounded by my faith background. Growing up in a Christian, Pentecostal environment, divorce was taught as the unpardonable sin—a mark of shame, something God looked upon with clear disapproval.

My brand, Fearfully & Wonderfully Made, is built to dismantle that theology of shame. I have learned that a broken marriage does not make one a broken person in God's eyes.

Our value is not tied to relationship status; it is secured in the truth of our divine creation. I want to help women move past the false guilt and into the boundless grace that affirms us that we are, in fact, wonderfully made, failure-free.

My ultimate mission is to inspire every woman to fully step into their role as a "Fearless Woman"—one who knows she can conquer the world because she walks hand-in-hand with her loving Heavenly Father.

I want women to fully understand that it is not about perfection. It's about wholeness.

Why I Am Sharing My Story

For a long time, I struggled to understand Psalm 119:71, "It was good that I was afflicted." There was nothing "good" about walking through heartbreak or the loneliness that followed my divorce. But over time, I began to see that even my hardest seasons had purpose. They revealed the gifts God had already placed in me—the same gifts I am now using to help others.

My journey through divorce tested everything I believed about faith, worth, and resilience. I had to learn how to start over, how to carry responsibility for my children, and how to rebuild my confidence one small step at a time. It was a painful process, but it also became the foundation for what God was preparing me to do next.

For more than four decades, I have worked in the insurance industry. My role as an underwriter requires patience, discernment, and precision—but it was through that same work that I discovered another passion. When new assistants joined the department, they were assigned to me for training.

I enjoyed helping them grow, explaining the details of policies, and watching them develop the confidence to succeed. Their progress gave me joy and fulfillment, and without realizing it, I was already walking in my calling to teach and mentor.

That same gift eventually opened a new door. When an individual outside my workplace struggled to pass their insurance exams, a colleague referred them to me. I agreed to help, using the same practical, hands-on approach that proved effective with those I had worked with in the past. I guided her to success.

What began as helping a few people quickly grew into steady requests for tutoring. I had not set out to start anything—I simply loved helping people understand what they once found difficult. But the results spoke for themselves, and before long, people were offering to compensate me for my time.

It was then I realized that God had been guiding me toward this all along. The ability to break complex information into simple terms, the joy I felt when someone succeeded, the quiet patience I had developed through my own trials—all of it had purpose. The same perseverance that carried me through personal hardship was now helping others overcome their own challenges.

This is why I share my story. Because every painful season carries a lesson that now serves someone else. My experience as a single mother taught me discipline. My professional journey taught me patience. My healing taught me compassion. And all of it together taught me that our purpose is never wasted—God uses every chapter.

As I prepare for the next stage of my life, I see this work not just as something I do, but as something I am called to continue. Tutoring and mentoring allow me to give back while walking in alignment with my faith. It is something I plan to grow even more in my retirement years not just as a source of income, but as a source of impact.

My story isn't about loss anymore—it's about legacy.

What once broke me now builds others.

And for that, I can finally say with peace in my heart: it was good that I was afflicted.

The Power of Mentorship

Titus 2:4–6 is more than a passage on spiritual living—it is God's model for generational strength. It reminds us that no woman heals in isolation. We rise when we share what we have learned.

I am a product of that principle. The wisdom of older women who poured into me did not just encourage me—it refined me. They reminded me that faith and fortitude could coexist with vulnerability. Their mentorship did not erase my pain; it gave it purpose.

Still, I learned that mentorship alone was not enough. True wholeness required both faith and follow-through. The women who spoke into my life gave me direction, but professional counseling gave me depth.

Mentorship nurtures the heart, while therapy strengthens the mind. One gives you vision; the other teaches you to sustain it. Together, they form the bridge from survival to restoration.

Now, I find myself on the other side of that bridge—mentoring others the same way I was once mentored. Through my work in the insurance field, tutoring professionals for their exams, and training new staff, I discovered that mentorship is not confined to ministry. It happens in boardrooms, classrooms, and everyday conversations.

For me, teaching has never been just about information; it is about transformation. I have seen how a little confidence can change everything. The same way my mentors breathed courage into me, I now help others silence self-doubt, sharpen their gifts, and show up with excellence.

Every challenge I faced—every setback and delay—was preparing me to pour into others with empathy and clarity. That's what Titus 2 really means to me: turning our experience into someone else's endurance.

Mentorship is the divine cycle of redemption. We are healed, so we can help heal. We are taught, so we can teach. We are strengthened, so we can lift. That's how God ensures that wisdom never dies—it simply changes hands.

Seeds & Bloom: What I Want You to Take With You

Every woman's life produces both ashes and beauty. What we plant in those ashes determines what blooms next. The lessons that shaped me were not learned in comfort—they were cultivated in brokenness, watered by tears, and grown through faith and hard work. These are my SEEDS—the truths I want to plant in you.

S – Self-Worth Beyond Roles

I want you to understand that when we base our identity on external factors—being in a relationship, motherhood, a career, or even a fit body—those things do not define us. They are enhancements, not our essence. When they fade or fail, God invites you to rediscover who you truly are—His masterpiece, loved and chosen.

E – Empathy and Encouragement

I know what it feels like to have nothing in the pantry and no one to call. That's why I am committed to being a steady support for others walking through their own valleys. Resilience and empathy are at the core of who I am. Healing happens when we refuse to suffer in silence and instead stand shoulder to shoulder with others.

E – Excavation Through Brokenness

I had to be truly broken to find the strength and self-worth I had long ignored. That breaking was not punishment—it was excavation. God was not destroying me; He was revealing me. The breakdown was the breakthrough.

D – Discipline in Faith and Action

It is not enough to simply know you are worthy—the faith piece. You must also rebuild your life through action: seeking help, saving wisely, learning new skills, and believing again when progress feels slow. Spiritual anchoring and practical effort go hand in hand.

S – Support and Sisterhood

No one heals in isolation. I am passionate about standing up for those who feel alone, offering tangible help, and reminding women that we are stronger when we walk together. Sisterhood is sacred—it is how God helps us heal.

And when those seeds take root, they grow into a beautiful BLOOM—a life of confidence, courage, and calling.

B – Bold Faith

I want you to feel empowered, to believe in the healing power of God, and to live with spiritual boldness. Let faith be the foundation for every step forward.

L – Liberation From the Past

True freedom comes when you stop letting what broke you define who you are. God redeems pain and turns it into purpose. You are not what happened to you—you are what He is doing through you.

O – Ownership of the Real You

I did not find a new me—I found the real me. The one who could lead, provide, and trust God without reservation. You can do the same. Own your story. Own your voice. Own your strength.

O – Overflowing Confidence

Walk into every room with quiet assurance—not arrogance, but anchored confidence. You are God's masterpiece—flawed and fabulous, chosen and complete. You don't need to shrink back when you were made to shine.

M – Mentorship in Motion

What God does in you is never just for you. Share it. Speak it. Pour it forward. Your healing becomes someone else's hope when you teach them how to bloom.

These are my SEEDS and my BLOOM—truths born from pain but perfected through grace.

If you plant them in your own life, they will grow into courage, confidence, and unshakable faith.

I chose pink as the color that represents my rose in bloom because it embodies grace and grit—the blend of gentleness and power that defines healed femininity.

It's the color of compassion that refuses to weaken, of love that's both tender and tenacious. Pink reminds me that I can be soft and strong, humble and bold, healed and still healing.

So wherever you are right now—whether rebuilding, rediscovering, or simply holding on—know this: You are still growing. You are still becoming. And when the time is right, you will bloom again—stronger, wiser, and more radiant than before.

Because you, too, are fearfully and wonderfully made.

To my mother & grandmother,

Nellie Brooks

&

Firstena Christie

(July 23, 1914 - February 9, 2009)

You shaped me with faith and fortified me with love.

Because of you, I am fearless, wonderfully rooted in purpose, and ready to bloom where I am planted.

When Plans Become Purpose

MICHAELLA ANN FORBES

THE THEATRE WAS PACKED, and camera lights flashed everywhere as photographers sought to capture photos of the "who's who" in the elegantly and glittered dressed audience.

I sat up straight in my seat, my body rigid, and breath baited, as the nominees were being announced. The rush of blood pounding in my ears was loud...so loud that I could barely hear the voices of the presenters.

"And the Oscar goes to..." the male presenter began.

There was a long, dramatic pause as his female co-host opened the white, 5 x 7 envelope. A hush fell over the theatre as the audience waited and looked on. I closed my eyes and made a fist with both hands.

Then I heard it. "Michaella Ann Forbes, for When Things Don't Go as Planned."

The words seemed to come from far away and echoed in the distance. Shock and disbelief filled me even as the room erupted in thunderous applause. I opened my eyes to see the audience around me on its feet...and all eyes were on me.

Is this real? It could be. The events of my life have certainly played out like a movie on the silver screen. It is complete with all the elements: love, heartbreak, disappointment, and a struggle of survival, all of which help to bring about a firm realization of who I am, and whose I am, birthing purpose in my life.

In my story, you will see a determined young girl who grew into a woman, all the while trying to do things my way, and as a result, encountering many hardships and disappointments, until I learned that it is God who is in control, and I needed to surrender my will to His.

I share my story so that other women with shared experiences will be inspired and know that they too can heal, grow and be restored, and then go on to become an inspiration to someone else. Let's go to where it all began, then at the end, cast your vote for best picture.

The Making of a Planner

The fingers on my hand were shorter than other kids from the very start. I was born to a single, teenage mother who almost did not graduate from high school because she entered motherhood at seventeen. She walked down the graduation aisle pregnant with my sister and then I was her second and last child born two years later.

My father was not present, physically or financially. It was just my mother, and she worked hard, coming home at weird hours so that she could provide for us. Seeing her struggle for us made me determined to do well—for her, and for myself. I wanted to go beyond what she had accomplished. She didn't have the opportunity to go to college, so I made up my mind that I would.

I was very young, a mere eight years old when I knew that I wanted to be the smartest person in my grade six graduating class. I calculated that to achieve my goal, I had to study more than the other kids so I could get perfect grades. So, I began to plan.

Planning has always come naturally to me, and where I felt most comfortable. It gave me a sense of control. I felt that if I planned it, I could then depend on it. I believe that the deep desire I developed to be in control at a young age arose because of an absent father in my life. He was not there for me to depend on or to give me that sense of assurance and security that every child needs to have and looks to their dad for.

I couldn't leave my future in anyone else's hands but mine, so early in life I earnestly planned my goals, how I would achieve them, what my life would look like and how I would save and spend my money. I remember planning weeks in advance for school fun days and special occasions like my mom's birthday or Mother's Day.

My grade six graduation came, and I was sure that I had executed my plans perfectly and was going to get the desired results. To my surprise, and disappointment, however, the top achiever award went to a boy instead of me. I remember asking my teacher how it had been possible for, let's call him Bobby, to get the award and not me, when my grades were better than his.

Her response was that even though I was smarter, she believed that a man should be the head of the household and thus the head of the class. That was my first heartbreak, but instead of allowing it to discourage me, I became obsessed with being the best academically. I wanted to do so well that there would be no room or opportunity for anyone to deny my accomplishments.

Valedictorian and Plan B

At that point, I began planning my next goal. I decided that when I graduated high school, I would be valedictorian of my graduating class even if that meant no extracurricular activities and no boys (because a boy got the award, and I didn't). I succeeded on the 'no extracurricular activities' but not so much for the 'no boys'.

All through high school I didn't participate in most of the extracurricular activities like sports that my classmates and other students were involved in. Instead, I immersed myself in my studies and I fought for and achieved, becoming the Valedictorian of my graduating class in 1997.

I remember it being one of the proudest moments in my life. It reinforced the value of planning and set a tone for me that I could set a goal, long term or short, plan out what I would do each day to achieve it and stick to it, then I would have success.

I was convinced that having a perfect plan was the way to go for the rest of my life and in every area of my life. Despite that conviction, some things still fell through the cracks. Notwithstanding not allowing myself time for anything outside of my studies in high school, I did however have an interest that was burning in my soul.

Yes, I wanted to excel academically, but my dream career was not a traditional one. What I wanted more than anything was to be an actress or a dancer. Being on stage was the only thing I made time for every once in a while other than my studies.

Back then I lived for the applause, and my choice of being an actress was not popular with those around me. There was no excitement over the prospect of my becoming an actress, however the responses were different when I spoke about accounting, and more and more I was led in that direction.

Choosing the "Safe" Path

Thirty years ago Bahamians did not look at acting as a viable career. My teachers and everyone I spoke to about becoming an actress either ignored what I said or tried to push me in another direction.

My own mother who I knew loved me deeply didn't even share in my dream, but now as a parent I acknowledge that it is understandable why she could not see the vision.

I believe in her heart she wanted me to have and achieve more than she had, and she could not see that happening with my first choice of a career on stage. I remember her asking me at one point what I wanted to do.

When I told her I wanted to be an actress or dancer. Without commenting on what I said, she asked me what my second selection was. I was good at numbers and felt that if I could not get into acting, accounting would be my second choice.

I told my mother this, and we agreed that accounting was what I would do. Still, my real love for the stage remained.

After high school, my mom helped me to pursue my studies in accounting. I became a Certified Public Accountant and a Chartered Financial Analyst and now have over twenty years of work experience in this field. Plan B had become Plan A, and I had succeeded in accomplishing it.

I should have been happy and content because my life was going as planned, but as I matured and became more grounded in my faith, I began to feel a stirring deep within me that accounting, though very beneficial in teaching me valuable lessons, was not what God had called me to be.

A Creative Hidden in Plain Sight

I can't say what, if anything, played a role in the birth of my creativity, but I do know that some things are learnt, while other things are inbred. According to my sister, my creativity and ability to tell stories is a gift from God. Ironically though, she is only now seeing it that way. She says that from her earliest memories of me, I've always been a creative, telling exaggerated stories that she confessed she found annoying at the time.

In my late twenties, I became heavily focused on trying new things and seeking to find my passion. In my search, I found a church home at Bahamas Harvest, a church here in Nassau, Bahamas. I joined the church's dance, and drama ministries respectively.

As I got involved in these areas, I was reminded of my primary school days when I had acted in and casted all my friends in a Bahamian version of my favorite movie, Annie. It was a fifth-grade performance done in class for our teacher, and I remembered how much I had loved it. That memory helped me to reconnect with my love of creating characters and exaggerating a story.

In the drama ministry at Bahamas Harvest Church, I played the lead role in a play called Storm Proof. Ironically, or maybe not, this story was about to become real to me. In our journey of faith there is nothing that is coincidental, ironic or accidental.

God has a purpose for everything that we go through. He takes the difficult circumstances that Satan tries to trip us with and uses them for our good. The play was staged as I was about to go through a personal storm that rocked my world and tested my marriage to the limit.

Love, Control, and the Timeline

Marriage. I was married at that time—yes—but my marriage was not the storm...not that storm. My father was not in my life practically all my adolescent years, and without a father or positive fatherly figure to love me, guide me, and protect me, and without understanding the effect of that void, I began looking for that love at an early age.

I was just 13 years old when I started dating, without my mother's permission of course. I knew that she loved me, and although I felt her love, I craved love from a man, and it led to me going from one romantic relationship to another as quickly as possible with no breaks in between.

Since my father obviously didn't want me in his life, I decided that I didn't need his name either. My mother had given me his surname, but I did not want to be associated with someone who did not want me, so at ten years old, I began trying to change it.

I had a stepfather who, unfortunately, was also very far from a model father, but I desperately wanted a different last name so I asked him if he would adopt me, without telling him why. I made this request in the early days of his marriage to my mother, but things quickly changed between them, and he became another negative father figure who I didn't want my name associated with.

That ended my strategy of changing my name through adoption, but I was the master planner and therefore was never without a new one. When the path of adoption didn't work, I set my eyes and my heart very early on marriage. To my young mind, singleness was not an option for me and marriage was the only viable path.

Looking back on my life and relationships, I really thought I was in love with each person I dated, but I know now that I did not have the slightest idea what love was. I realize that I felt what I told myself to feel, and it was all a part of me trying to control what happened in my life in order for me to gain a certain outcome.

My plan was to go to the local college in The Bahamas right after high school, then relocate to a University in Florida and get my bachelor's degree in accounting by the age of twenty-two, have a promising career as a Certified Public Accountant by twenty-four, married to the love of my life by twenty-five, and have two extremely smart kids (GIRLS) by twenty-nine.

Little did I know, the person I thought was the love of my life (the last piece of the puzzle) was not ready to get married after six years of dating, and our relationship ended badly when I was twenty-four.

I was heartbroken, probably the most heartbroken I have ever been over a breakup, but I suppressed the pain, and in two weeks I moved on to another relationship. Singleness was still not an option, and I needed to stick to the timeline I had created in my head.

Not once did I stop to ask God what His plans for me were. It did not occur to me at all to do so. I was on a mission. Planning had worked well so far, so I just needed to press a little harder and I would reach my goal. I eventually got married at twenty-seven, finally changed my last name, and had both of my kids by age thirty. This was not exactly the timeline I had laid out, but it was not far from it and my name was no longer 'Rolle".

When the Plan Includes a Son

As I mentioned previously, in my plan, my two children would be girls. In my mind, I was going to have two girls. I prayed for it and envisioned us becoming the second generation, three musketeer girl power team like I perceived my mother, my sister and I to be. I became pregnant—the plan was going well.

Then, wait. What? I was having a boy. When I found out, I was quite disappointed. What was I going to do with a boy I thought? That was not the plan! I tried to picture how a male figure, or a little boy would fit into my immediate family with little or no positive male role models. All my childhood memories were flooded with strong, female figures and to say I was less than excited was an understatement.

When my son came into this world, I loved him dearly but still struggled with raising a boy in the right way because I had never seen it done. I never saw a boy being raised in my family, and more importantly, I could not relate to the things he wanted to do. He wanted to crash trucks instead of having a tea party with dolls. He wanted to jump off countertops instead of playing dress up.

Even shopping for a boy seemed quite dull because I had to pass the various cute girly outfits on my way to the basic boy section with fewer options. Little did I know, this little boy would change me and make me want to be a better woman in a different way. God had given me what He knew I needed, and not what I wanted.

Being around many strong women inspired me to be tough but my son would inspire me to be a little softer. Even though I struggled with relationships with men, he inspired me to think about the words I spoke over him because one day he would grow up to be a man and I would want positivity spoken over him. He inspired me to learn how to handle my emotions because he was watching, and his personality was becoming like mine even though I did not see it working well within a male.

A Storm, a Stage, and a One-Pound Miracle

I became pregnant with my second child, and this time, God saw fit to bless me with the little girl I always wanted. Even though I planned to have her, her coming into the world the way she did was very spontaneous and scary.

I was almost six months pregnant and the lead actress in a drama at my church called Storm Proof. The drama was about a mother who went through storm after storm in her life. Little did I know that within a few hours of leaving that stage, I too would go through one of the toughest times in my life. The production was on a Sunday morning.

By mid-day I started to have very excruciating pain. I thought I was having cramps but as the pain intensified, I thought it best to go to the hospital. I got there at 4 p.m. and my water broke as soon as I walked through the doors. Everything was happening quickly. My daughter was about to be born, whether I was ready or not!

She was born on October 3rd, 2010, weighing one pound. Her lungs were not fully developed, so she had to be connected to tubes to breathe with the assistance of a machine. For the next four months following her birth, she had many blood transfusions and there were many scares of her heart stopping.

During the time my daughter was in hospital, I also had to be hospitalized because the doctor who delivered her did not remove the afterbirth. That, coupled with the fact that after my daughter's birth, I went back to work too soon to compensate for her not being home and my marriage falling apart right in front of my eyes.

As a result, I overworked myself and collapsed at the office and had to be hospitalized for four days. It was a difficult season in my life, but it was also the time when my faith in God was challenged as I finally experienced Him for myself for the first time and my relationship with Him was made real to me. My daughter took a breath on her own for the first time on Christmas day 2010, and I knew then that it was God, and that miracles still exist!

Cracks in the Marriage

My daughter remained in the hospital for four months, and that season challenged not only my faith, but many other areas of my life as well—my physical strength, my mental capacity, and my multitasking skills—and not the least of them, it tested my already troubled marriage.

As those months brought me closer to God, my husband on the other hand was stricken with a fear of death and chose to be absent physically from me as his wife. He also rarely visited our daughter in the hospital. One week after she was born, he decided to go abroad to study and take certifications instead of being there for his family.

It was that week when I collapsed, but he chose not to come home, and that broke my heart. It was an emotional test that should have brought us closer, but instead it created a distance that lasted for years and I would not know how to fix it.

My marriage was in trouble. We were emotionally struggling before this because his main focus seemed to be on making money instead of his family, and although we went through counseling, the only thing we shared was silence.

The silence grew louder and louder as time passed and even though he had always been quiet, our relationship almost became cold. Me? I became superwoman for my children because I realized that I could not trust him to have my back nor the children's like I had envisioned.

My daughter finally came home from the hospital on February 7th, 2011, so tiny and weighing only 3.5 pounds but in excellent health physically. My mother joked that my daughter came early because she wanted to be born in her own month as opposed to November through March when all the rest of her immediate family were born. She had overcome her challenges...or so we thought.

Lessons from My Miracle Girl

Later in her toddler years, she was diagnosed with ADD (Attention Deficit Disorder) which affects her memory and the way she learns. I was a straight-A student and envisioned that with my help and planning, my children would be the same, but this was not the case for my precious, little, miracle, baby girl that I prayed for.

My little girl has taught me to look deeper than grades to her gifts, and discover what God's purpose is for her life and not my own. The experience of her premature birth took my faith in God to another level and turned that test into a testimony about His miracles.

Her personality was the opposite of mine, and she has taught me that I can plan in my head as much as I want, but that some things are out of my control as she would rather wear a hoodie and baggy pants than a cute, girly, pink dress that would match mine and make us twins.

When My Plans Collapsed

"For I know the plan I have for you," declares the Lord and this is a promise that I believe and stand on. My faith is wrapped up in the belief that God is forever standing with me, and everything that has happened to me has been for a reason and for a purpose. Some of what I endured was because I sought to live my life my way instead of choosing to seek God, be still and allow Him to show me what His plans were for my life but God!

Because of this, God allowed me to see the error in my ways and learn that even though some of my plans did not work out as calculated, He was and is still gracious and merciful enough to use those broken, painful things, to create a beautiful tapestry in my life. He is showing me how to use the pain and create purpose. I have "Plans to prosper you and not to harm you".

My life experiences have given me much material for the gift that God has placed in me—to write, act, produce and create. I am better at these things now because of what I came through. ...plans to give you hope and a future.

Between the time my daughter was born in 2010 and 2021, I had gone through two separations and two infidelities within my marriage. When I left in 2021, I knew it would be hard, but it was the first time that choosing uncertainty (no plans) became a better option for my life. At that time, I was completely depressed, utterly depleted and could not even muster the energy to plan at all.

All I could do was cling on to a voice inside telling me that I desperately needed to do something to save myself. In the past, I could always gather up enough passion and fight with everything in me to show up again, but this time it was all gone, and it sucked the joy out of everything else good in my life.

I did not have the mental or emotional capacity to consider my children, the house, our family or friends, my church, my art, or worry about what others would think.

I just knew I could not remain in an emotionally starved and distant marriage one day longer without risking completely losing myself to the point of no return. I had to get out of the environment and trust that God would make a way as long as I took the first step.

While separated, I went on a 40 day fast during Easter of 2021 and I prayed for clarity, and during that time the Holy Spirit released me from my marriage. Shortly after this release, the same voice told me to stop renting and move back into the marriage home where my then husband still resided which confused me so I did not act on it right away. For about two weeks I ignored the voice of The Holy Spirit until the disobedience became uncomfortable.

I reluctantly returned home, wondering at first if I heard wrong the first time and maybe God has not actually released me. However, upon re-entering the doors; it became clearer and clearer that the marriage was dead.

The coldness and the silence was even more deafening than I remembered and for weeks we said nothing and I eventually broke the silence in tears and said to him (my husband at the time) all that was on my mind and in my heart, holding nothing back. He had no empathy for my tears and walked away.

When I was finished with that communication, the Holy Spirit said even louder, "Now you are completely released."There were times in the past after I started to heal within the marriage that I would pray very hard that God would change my husband's heart towards me and allow him to show up in a big emotional way for our marriage and our family, which would be out of character for him and would give some glimmer of hope in my mind for a future. But it never happened.

We got divorced in August of 2022 and I never looked back.

The fast in 2021 was a pivotal point in my life. It was the time I added fasting to praying and became serious about seeking God's plans, and asking His direction, instead of presenting Him with my plans, and asking Him to bless them.

Because I really surrendered my life to His leading, He began to direct me and make changes in my life. Apart from receiving directions for my marriage during the fast, my love of writing, especially journalling was deepened.

At that time God also made it quite clear to me that the next phase of my life was a healing phase and I needed to for the first time in a very long time (remember I was in and out of relationships since the age of thirteen) and for a minimum of a year be by myself, not even entertaining the opposite sex for conversation.

This turned out to be one of the best decisions of my life because the fear I had of being alone was now transformed into an even deeper faith in the plans that my Father had for me. I started to re-discover myself and day after day all my joy, peace and hope were not only returned but magnified.

As I am writing this, it has been three years post divorce and this single season has allowed me to dive deeper into what my purpose is and pursue it unapologetically. God has promised that remarriage is in my future and I am resting on His word that, "When the time is right, HE (not me) will make it happen."

A Letter to My Father

I spent the rest of 2021 after my final separation in individual counseling and discovered that I still had a lot of anger, hurt and pain toward my father. It was in counseling that I was instructed to write him a letter since I loved to write.

For me it was an easy letter to write but I had no intention of giving it to him because I feared he would be angry or worse, not respond, pretending he never read it.

I kept it in my Bible for all of 2021, and finally gave it to him in early 2022. What happened was not what I expected at all. My father was not only ready to receive the letter, but he also apologized to both me and my mom for being absent. Now, for the first time, he and I are beginning to forge a friendship.

Sometimes—no, most times, the things we fear the most are covered up with the unknown. Sometimes too, we allow our lives to be affected by the fears and uncertainties of others, but I have learned, and am continuing to learn, that I don't have to fear the unknown, or the future for that matter, and not to allow other people's fears to govern my life, because God already has it all worked out for me.

I allowed people's views of my desire to be an actress to determine the career I would choose all those years ago. I stopped writing and pursuing stage in high school to choose a more predictable path but now I am giving wings to my creativity and allowing God to utilize the gift He gave me in any way He sees fit because I trust Him.

Returning to the Page and the Stage

In 2022, I wrote and released my song Invisible Wounds, as well as a short film called Distant, all based on my life. My film won a few awards from various film festivals that year and was chosen to be showcased at Bahamas Film Festival 2023.

My writing has always been an important part of my life, and as I look back, it has always been that constant, and the thing that God used to bring healing to me in various seasons and experiences.

I remember the day God told me, through the Holy Spirit, to begin writing again. It was 2016. I was driving, and God began to reveal to me that I had unresolved issues from a previous relationship, and told me to write a play about it. I resisted the prompting at first but eventually gave in as the request became more persistent. I pulled on the side of the road and began to write.

That was my reintroduction to writing. A year later in 2017, I wrote, directed, produced and acted in my stage play called "All of Me"at The Dundas Theater. It was an emotional drama about finding yourself, and life knocking you down as you discover who you really are.

The protagonist was a young girl, Tamika, whose heart was broken by her first true love, Brian, who was also her best friend and the man she thought she would marry.

Tamika tries to put her life back together and move on but can't fully give all of herself to another because she is broken. She is torn by what her heart wants to do, what she knows is the right thing to do, and what others think she should do. She eventually turns to God, and he turns her mess into a message of hope.

I wrote the play so I could begin my healing process. It was staged again at my church by request for a Singles Series in 2018, at the Bahamas Bridal Show in 2019, and was nominated for a Bahamian Icon Award.

During this time, I had also become very involved in ministry, although not the drama ministry. I was leader of the Imag (image) ministry, and I controlled all the images and videos on screen during church services.

I chose that instead of the drama ministry because drama was too time demanding during the week with two small babies. But by 2018, I was ready to leave the Imag ministry and lead the drama ministry at my church because I knew my calling was linked to drama and creativity.

It was in the drama ministry that I honed my craft and wrote and directed many productions for the Kingdom of God. I also joined the acting community with my first audition for the play For Colored Girls where I was chosen for the part of Green who recited the poem "Somebody almost walked off with all my stuff," a poem that represented my life at the time. That role led to many others in the community, and I even directed some short plays.

Healing Through Art and Obedience

In 2020, during the time of isolation and lockdowns of the COVID-19 Pandemic, I pressed into my relationship with God more and realized that He loved me so much and wanted me to live a life of abundance in all areas, even relationally.

I turned forty in December 2020, and I decided that I would enjoy life no matter what and threw myself a 40th birthday party despite the broken state of my marriage at that time. I wrote a rap song called, "I Just Wanna Be Me and Everything God has Called Me to Be" and performed it at my 40th birthday party. These words I would hold onto for the next few months as I went through separation.

From 2021 to 2024, while serving as drama leader at Bahamas Harvest Church, I directed the Easter production each year: The Truth, The Great Reset and The Crucifixion. In 2024, I co-authored an Anthology book entitled, Golden Key by writing the chapter titled The Artistic Accountant.

My latest venture has been to bring a vision God gave me early 2024 to life of a stage play (The Affair) that shows that some marriages with adultery may end in divorce but some through Him find healing and purpose.

I co-produced this play with Bahamian Icon winner Kerel Pinder who wrote it as I directed it. The play had three showings in Nassau, New Providence in early November, 2024 and February 2025 respectively, and two showings in Freeport, Grand Bahama in late November 2024.

Writing was helping me heal from the loss of my marriage. Divorce is that—a loss—but I wanted to be sure that I was healing properly so I joined a group called Divorce Care recommended by my sister.

It was the best decision at the time, as being a part of an intimate group of ladies going through similar struggles proved to be life changing.

Being in the program and hearing the similar stories of other resilient women who went through the same pain made me feel connected to a purpose and less alone. I was able to open up to the group about all aspects of my life, but little did I know, this would catapult me in a direction I did not see coming.

In 2023, I began to be led by the Holy Spirit to create a place where other divorced/separated persons could feel what I felt in Divorce Care, and my podcast, "A Safe Space," was launched in October of 2023 along with me leading healing after divorce groups within my church.

My hope is that my podcast and the circles formed within these groups become a place where others will feel comfortable and secure enough to share their stories, heal, grow and be restored and their stories will encourage and inspire others.

More than that my hope is that both spaces becomes all that God has purposed for it and that He will direct my path.

Single Again, But Not Alone

As I write this chapter in 2025, I am now 45, divorced and single (not in a relationship) for the first time in my adult life which was not part of the plan. I don't think anyone goes into marriage thinking they will end up divorced, however, divorce has become my reality.

The girl who used to plan most of her life in advance had now reached a point where planning or even focusing too much on the future brought me anxiety and I could only find the strength to live for the present.

I now understand why the "Our Father Prayer" says, give us our daily bread because today is all we really need and when we put tomorrow in God's hand and embrace the present, it can become a gift.

This time in my life that I call "single again" has caused me to reflect on and gain clarity about so many things and aspects of my life. Being single again has sparked a healing process that even I could not have imagined, and now I am so much hungrier to know God at a more intimate level!

I never thought I could truly be happy single, but it has helped me to get to know who Michaella truly is without the title of wife, mother, CPA or any role; just me, liking my company, letting go of control (letting go of the need to know exactly how things will turn out), trying new things, and allowing myself to relax and be.

Through my healing, I have come to like who I am and to trust God with my life and the things that concern me. Even though the experiences were painful, they allowed me to grow and discover myself, and that lead to me finding my purpose.

I finally learned the beauty of the word "and" which allowed me to dig deeper into my artistic side and embrace it to blending with the accounting part of me instead of thinking I had to5 choose between them.

Redeemed Plans: The Financially Creative Coach

After everything I had been through—the heartbreak, the losses, the rebuilding—the one thing that remained constant was my career. My job had been my anchor, my safe place, my source of identity and provision.

When life felt uncertain, work was the one area I could still control. Through all the turmoil, I kept showing up, performing, excelling, and planning my next professional milestone. It gave me stability when everything else around me seemed to shift like sand.

But lo and behold—not even two years after my divorce, just when I thought I had finally found my rhythm again, the winds of change in my life began to blow once more. It was early 2024 when I first began to sense it.

It wasn't loud or dramatic—just a quiet stirring deep within me that I couldn't quite shake. I started to feel a divine uneasiness, like God was whispering that there was more for me beyond the four walls of my office.

At first, I tried to ignore it. After all, I had worked hard to build this stability in my career. I had already endured enough uncertainty for a lifetime—why would God ask me to let go of the one thing in my life that felt secure? But the more I prayed, the more I realized it wasn't my imagination. God was shifting something.

I resisted at first. I told Him I wasn't ready, that the timing wasn't right, that maybe this feeling would pass. But His voice became clearer: "It's time to prepare for what I've prepared for you." So, I did what I've always done best—I made a plan. But this time, I didn't plan out of fear. I planned out of faith.

I began transitioning to entrepreneurship for over a year before the date He would later reveal as my full release from corporate employment. I spent months praying, fasting, and listening for His direction. Every decision became a conversation with God. I mapped out my finances, created a runway, increased passive investment income, decreased expenses, saved intentionally, and outlined a timeline—not to control the outcome, but to steward the process well.

Slowly, I began to see the purpose in the planning. God wasn't asking me to abandon the structure He had gifted me with; He was teaching me to submit it back to Him. I learned that planning without partnership is just performance. But when you let God lead the process, planning becomes prophecy. He began to realign everything.

The same skills I used for decades in my career as a CPA and CFA—forecasting, managing, preparing—were now tools for building something Kingdom-centered and creative. The more I prayed, the clearer it became that God was birthing something new in me: a business, a ministry, and a movement.

By mid-2025, peace had replaced the fear. I knew my release was near, and when the Holy Spirit finally told me it was time to write my resignation letter, I cried—not out of sadness, but out of gratitude. Gratitude that God had trusted me enough to redirect me. Gratitude that I had learned to trust Him enough to follow. My last day as a corporate employee was October 31, 2025. The very next day—November 1, 2025—I officially stepped into full-time entrepreneurship and purpose.

That transition wasn't impulsive; it was intentional. It was the fulfillment of a year of obedience and preparation. I didn't leap blindly—I walked boldly. I left one chapter with wisdom and entered the next with worship. And the moment I took that step, everything in my spirit said, This is what you were created for.

I now rest on Jeremiah 29:11: "For I know the plans I have for you," declares the Lord, "plans to prosper you and not to harm you, plans to give you hope and a future." Though I still believe in the value of planning, I have learned to stop over-planning, because I now know that God's plan is always better than mine could ever be. What I once used as a tool for control has now become an instrument of purpose.

In seeking Him, I have evolved into The Financially Creative Coach—a woman who merges faith, finance, and freedom. Through my Page-to-Stage Method, I help women who are transitioning after a major life change or loss, create the abundant life God promised them. I teach them how to find or rediscover themselves, plan projects with precision, steward resources with wisdom, and build purpose with profit.

As an artistic accountant, I walk women through blending the black-and-white world of budgeting, planning, and structure with the colorful world of storytelling, creativity, and divine calling. Together, we build something lasting—not from fear, but from faith.

Now, planning is no longer my idol; it's my ministry. I no longer plan to protect myself. I plan to prepare for God's promises. I no longer chase deadlines. I follow divine direction.

If you are standing where I once stood—comfortable, yet restless—know that obedience will always take you further than comfort ever could. Let me, the artistic accountant, walk with you through this same journey of becoming.

Visit my biography and website, and let's start this partnership that can lead you into the authentic, abundant life you were always meant to live. Because when you truly surrender your plans to God, He doesn't take away your dreams—He refines them until they align with His purpose for your life.

Why I Wrote My Story

I chose to share my story because silence had kept me bound for far too long. For years, I wore strength like armor, telling myself that if I just kept moving, planning, and performing, I would eventually outrun the pain. But healing doesn't happen in hiding—it happens in honesty.

When I began to speak openly about my journey—about divorce, disappointment, and rediscovering my worth—I realized that my vulnerability wasn't a weakness. It was a key. Every time I shared a part of my story, another woman found permission to face her own. That is why I continue to speak, to write, and to coach. I want women to know that even the most unplanned detours can still lead to destiny.

Ann Voskamp once wrote, "Shame dies when stories are shared in safe spaces." Those words became a truth I live by. My healing deepened when I stopped protecting my pain and started using it to build connections. What began as one woman's testimony became a bridge—a place where others could cross from brokenness to breakthrough. When I launched my podcast, A Safe Space, I had no idea how much healing would happen on both sides of the microphone. Each conversation became holy ground—women sharing, weeping, laughing, and realizing they were not alone.

When someone reaches out and tells me, "Your story gave me the courage to start again," it humbles me every single time. Those moments remind me that none of my pain was wasted. Every detour, every delay, every tear was preparation for this assignment—to help women rebuild with wisdom, purpose, and financial stability.

That's the heart behind everything I do now as The Financially Creative Coach. My story is the foundation, but my mission is the blueprint. I teach women—especially those who are "single again"—how to find peace in their finances, confidence in their creativity, and clarity in their calling.

Through my coaching programs, I merge strategy with spirituality: helping women move from survival to sustainability, from wishful thinking to wealth alignment. Because healing isn't just about feeling better—it's about building better.

I want every woman I encounter to know that God's plan for her life is still active, no matter what she's lost. She can start again, not from scratch, but from experience. And when she does, she won't just recover what she thought she lost—she'll rise with something greater: divine direction, renewed confidence, and the tools to thrive.

That's why I wrote my story. Not just to tell what I've been through, but to show what's possible when we let God rewrite the plan.

The Power of Mentorship

For a long time, I misunderstood what mentorship truly meant. In my early adult years, I believed a mentor had to be someone assigned to me at work—a supervisor, a boss, or someone older and more accomplished who would only step in if something went wrong in my career. I thought mentorship was strictly professional, reserved for formal settings, and limited to job titles and promotions.

But over time, and especially through my own healing and spiritual growth, God began to expand that definition. He showed me that mentorship is so much more than guidance for your résumé—it's nourishment for your becoming. It's not just about climbing a ladder; it's about building a life aligned with your divine purpose.

Some mentors teach through words. Others mentor by example, through how they live, give, and show up. And sometimes, God sends you mentors for a single season—just long enough to awaken a gift or remind you of who you are.

When I began to embrace my artistic side and feel whole within myself again, I found myself drawn to people who carried qualities I wanted to cultivate—peace, confidence, courage, faith, and creativity. I didn't always announce that they were my mentors. I simply positioned myself to learn from them. I volunteered to serve, to observe, to sit quietly in their space and absorb what they modeled. I became a student of their excellence.

That's when I discovered something life-changing: if you remain teachable, the right mentor can transfer years of wisdom into your weeks of readiness. A good mentor doesn't just teach you what to do—they help you see who you are.

Mentorship, when done right, multiplies purpose. It compresses time. It provides language for seasons you can't yet describe and strategies for challenges you didn't know how to face.

Through my own journey, I've realized that mentorship is one of the most powerful accelerators of transformation. It's why I now devote so much of my heart and energy to mentoring women through The Financially Creative Coach and my Page-to-Stage programs. My coaching is mentorship in motion—a space where I pour out what God has poured into me.

I help women bridge the gap between the spiritual and the practical—between the vision they see in prayer and the plan they must walk out in purpose. Whether it's mapping out finances, structuring a business, publishing a story, or rebuilding life after loss, mentorship helps them shorten the distance between pain and purpose.

I now understand that mentorship isn't about hierarchy—it's about legacy. It's about reaching back while reaching forward. It's about being humble enough to learn and generous enough to teach.

And if I've learned anything from this journey, it's this: We all need someone who has walked where we're heading—and we all carry something that can light the path for someone else.

From Seeds to Bloom

Looking back over my life, I can see that every experience—every heartbreak, every victory, every unexpected turn—was a seed God was planting.

For years, I tried to control the soil, the seasons, and the outcome through careful planning. Planning gave me comfort. It gave me direction. But as I matured in faith, I learned that the goal was never to plan perfectly—it was to plan prayerfully.

God used the detours to teach me dependence. He used the pauses to build patience. And when I thought I was standing still, He was cultivating the unseen roots of my purpose.

Now I understand that growth happens in two movements: sowing the SEEDS and allowing life to BLOOM.

S – Surrender

It is good to plan, but even better to remember that God's plan is always greater. True peace came when I surrendered the blueprint I created and allowed Him to draw the architecture of my life. I still plan—but I plan with open hands.

E – Embrace "And"

For years, I believed I had to choose: accountant or artist, logic or creativity, structure or spirit. God showed me that I was never meant to choose—I was meant to combine the words and set me free. You can be faithful and ambitious, strategic and surrendered, practical and prophetic. Wholeness can live in the *and.*

E – Excellence

Excellence is the fruit of stewardship. It's not about perfection; it's about honoring God by managing what He's entrusted to you—time, talents, finances, and opportunities. Every budget I built and every play I produced reminded me that excellence is worship in motion.

D – Deep Healing

Healing made space for the harvest. I could not bloom while clinging to brokenness.

When I allowed God to turn my pain into purpose, I realized that even the hard soil of disappointment can grow something divine.

S – Support and Stewardship

No one grows in isolation. I learned to pray for the right mentors, communities, and collaborations.

God answered with women who watered my faith and held space for my growth. Stewardship is not only about money—it's also about relationships, wisdom, and purpose.

Those were the SEEDS. Then came the BLOOM.

B – Believe God's Plan Is Better

Faith is the light that draws life from the soil. Even when things didn't go as planned, I learned to trust that His detours were still leading me toward destiny.

L – Learn Through the Layers

Every layer of my story—planning, pruning, waiting, surrendering—was a classroom. Growth takes time, and maturity requires patience.

O – Own Your Story

When I began to tell my story without shame, I found freedom. Ownership brings empowerment. Transparency plants courage in others.

O – Operate in Excellence

Excellence is not reserved for public stages; it's cultivated in private discipline. I now operate from purpose, not pressure, knowing that everything I do is a reflection of who God has called me to be.

M – Multiply What God Gave You

Every gift is meant to multiply. The wisdom I've gained, the skills I've honed, and the healing I've received are all seeds for someone else's growth. This is what legacy looks like—stewardship that multiplies impact.

Lime green, which is my favorite color, and the color I chose to represent my own rose in bloom, represents renewal, energy, and divine awakening. It's the color of new life breaking through old ground, a vivid reminder that restoration is real.

As I step fully into my calling as The Financially Creative Coach, I carry these lessons with me. My mission is to help other women, especially those who are single again, design lives that are abundant, structured, and spiritually aligned. I teach them how to plan with faith, steward with wisdom, and prosper with purpose.

So, if you take nothing else from my story, take this: Plan—but let God lead the plan. Embrace your *and*. Seek healing, and let Him turn your pain into purpose. Pray for mentors and community to walk beside you.

Because when you plant the right SEEDS and trust God with the BLOOM, you don't just rebuild...you rise.

To my mother,

Melanie Swaby

You taught me that strength isn't always loud, it's found in silence, prayer, and perseverance.

Because of you, I learned to endure with grace and to trust God's timing in every season.

Grace in every Season

Raquel Bain

I stood with my nose pressed against the window as I watched the family across the street. Every day I watched them come and go—the mom, the dad, and their two children: a boy and a girl. They were regular people, just as we were—Mom, Dad and I—except for one major difference, one that no one else could see and feel except me.

Time passes and scenes change. I'm grown now and no longer looking out of the window, but into a mirror, trying to recognize the woman looking back at me. This person is not who I envisioned I would become and in many ways and I feel like she is slowly disappearing.

Instead, I see the eyes of a stranger confused by her circumstances, their murky depths filled with pain.

On my lips and in my heart, an unspoken cry: *My God, my God, why hast Thou forsaken me? Why art Thou so far from helping me?*

I searched for what was missing from my childhood, but it did not end in a "happily ever after," and it was hard to understand why.

Foundations of Family and Faith

I was born to young, unmarried parents. My mother was nineteen and my father was twenty-one years old. They separated shortly after I was born, so I didn't start life with a father figure around.

Fortunately, I was too young to notice his absence. When I was seven years old, however, my mom got married to a man who would be a great father figure in my life.

Because I was so young when they got married, everyone else who did not know my mom and stepfather prior to their marriage also thought that he was my biological father. People considered him my father and gave me his last name automatically.

They would say *your dad*, *your daughter*, and we never corrected them. It was easy for them to come to that conclusion, too, as he never treated me as anything less than his daughter.

Although my stepfather and I shared a connection, I always knew that he was not my dad, and I secretly harbored a bit of jealousy towards children who lived in a home with both parents, where everyone had the same last name. I didn't have that.

Both my mom and my step-dad shared the same last name, but I had another, which made me feel like I was on the outside looking in.

When I had to write our names or when my name was called, I would be reminded that my name was different from my parents', and I felt that difference, but I chose never to voice that insecurity to anyone.

I do not know if my parents sensed how I felt and tried to compensate for it, or maybe it was just because I was an only child, but looking back, I guess it could be said that they spoiled me. My mother didn't have any other children after her marriage to my stepfather, and he did not have any of his own, so it was just the three of us.

We were not rich by any means, but I did not know what it was like to not have something. While my parents told me "no" at times, in retrospect, I realized that I generally got everything that I asked for. Particularly on the occasions of my birthday and Christmas, every year they told me to write my list. And no matter what was on it, no matter how crazy or outrageous, I always got my requests.

Sometimes they would give me a little push back, but even then I knew deep down I was going to get my wish. The year I turned eighteen, I asked for a car. My mom's response was (in her Bahaminese voice), "A car? Who does ask for a car? What do you think this is?!" But guess what? When my birthday came, I got the car.

I grew up thinking that getting what you wanted was normal, that it was the way everyone lived, and I think that belief shaped my thinking towards all relationships. In hindsight, I can see how that thinking manifested and permeated through my romantic life.

Men I dated would reiterate that I was spoiled and had to have things my way. It was true that I always wanted what I wanted, when I wanted it, but as they continually pointed out, that was not how it was supposed to be, but that was all I knew.

Yes, I may have been spoiled, but I believe that the environment I grew up in was largely responsible for nurturing my personality and creating in me my resilient spirit—a resilience that kept me in good stead after my life was turned upside down.

I had a warm, loving home which gave me a stable foundation, and allowed me to grow up feeling secure and confident. That encouraging environment was not limited to my immediate home either, but existed among my extended family on all sides. I had a great village.

I had a great church community as well. A strong faith and Christian heritage were an integral part of my foundation. My parents and I attended a conservative, old school church that was very Bible based, founded on, and rooted in the Word.

To complete my network of a strong base, I also attended a Christian school called Nassau Christian Academy. The school was incredibly small, so the environment was very intimate. There were only twelve children in my class at the most at any point in time for six years (grades seven to twelve), and I had the same classmates for my entire educational journey up to graduation.

My foundation was solid, and my self-esteem was high. I did not lack or feel in need of anything or anyone. My cup of love was full, so when I started to date, it was not because I necessarily needed a man in my life, but I figured it was that time and the guy who asked me out seemed interesting, so I consented.

However, I did not feel desperate and thought to myself if he chose not to call me anymore, and we never spoke again, it would be fine. Having a man in my life, even from such a young age, was never a priority.

I never felt diminished or less than for being alone, and I think it was that mindset that helped me to be strong when it came to the point where I had to divorce and let go of an unhealthy marriage and husband.

When Expectations Meet Reality

While my upbringing made me strong, it also made me naive enough to expect the same type of trouble-free environment that was in my upbringing in my marriage.

Growing up, of course, you'll have your ups and downs, but I was not expecting marriage to be as difficult as it was. I actually expected to ultimately receive the desires of my heart because I was a Christian, a virgin and I usually got what I wanted from my parents and my community who loved me. Slowly I came to realize that my reality would be almost the total opposite.

I learned after the fact that being unequally yoked doesn't solely have to do with being Christian vs non-Christian because my husband was a Christian as well, but we were not aligned in so many ways.

Our beliefs in terms of Christianity were different, as well as our backgrounds. Even how we thought and our values collided constantly, and it took me a while to come to terms with the fact that this was the life and the person I chose.

I have lived my life to seek out solutions to problems and situations and I tried to change my husband to do the same so we could make the marriage work. I was willing to do whatever it took because I wanted my children to have the same name as myself and my husband and not feel like an outsider.

I just always wanted that nuclear family life that I saw growing up, but at some point the cost became too high and I was unsuccessful.

When I finally came to terms with the fact that my marriage was not improving, I called my mother and told her that I didn't think I could make it in my marriage any longer.

I made up my mind at that point that it was going to be me and my two children, and that with God's help I was going to make it. I was going to raise my children by myself. It was not an easy decision as I always thought that when I got married it would be forever.

It was very difficult to come to grips with the loss and let go of that dream that I had for myself, my husband, and my children.

With the decision made, I was willing to work at raising my children on my own.

Building Stability in the Storm

My husband and I separated in 2012 before my youngest child turned one. At that time, my son (eldest) was four years old and had just been diagnosed with Autism.

I did not want to be a burden to my parents, so rather than moving back home, I moved into an apartment with my children. I had to make my income work for my little family.

All bills and care giving for my children were on me; a huge responsibility that I did not take lightly. I was determined to make a home for my children seeing that I was the parent who had initiated the separation. I thought that it was more my "fault" than his since I had "broken" the home physically.

After my husband and I separated, I knew I needed to have a plan for how I was going to create stability and a loving home for my children as a single parent. I wanted my children to participate in clubs and other activities with their peers.

I planned, and I believe I accomplished a great portion of that plan, but it was not easy. Making it work called for a lot of sacrifice; some I am still making.

Looking back, I can see that God was with me, and that He had His hands on my life. He opened doors, paved the way, and made things happen. He made the money work, but I didn't always see it that way.

Even while we were married, the children's father never supported me nor the children financially, and he certainly did not support us after the separation. My salary was my sole source of income.

My daughter had always attended private school, and because I did not want anything else in their life to change, I continued to pay school fees for her.

Also, my son is on the autism spectrum. When he was much younger, he had speech therapy, doctor's appointments, and different types of helping aids. It was recommended for him to play baseball to help with the dexterity of his hand.

Overall, my son's care was not cheap but even if it had been, my finances were so limited I had to stretch every dollar to the max.

But God was in the mix, directing every chord of the tune that was now my life. There was a yearly fee that had to be paid for my son to play baseball, however, through God's intervention, I never had to pay it.

The fee was never requested, and he was either given the uniform, or we were able purchase a secondhand one with donations from others.

I have watched God make things happen for us. I know it could not have been me because I only had so much. My salary could only go so far, and I watched Him turn the value of a dollar into $50, even into $100.

Despite me being the sole provider in my family, the bills have always been paid, the utilities have always been on, and my daughter has never been out of school for nonpayment of fees. I believe in all these things that God still saw me.

Scripture says that Christ saved me so that I can have life and have it more abundantly. I had to recognize that the marital situation I was in where there's absolutely no support, and no interest or effort to do better, was not the abundant life the bible speaks about.

Rather, it was more like being financially and emotionally abused, and I know that is not what my father in heaven or earth would want for me. I do not think it is the way God intended marriage to be, but neither do I believe that divorce is of Him, so I wrestled with indecision for a long time.

It took a while for me to get past the guilt and believe that even though I am not with my husband, that God still loves me, still has a plan for me, that my life is still meaningful, and I am not any less because I am no longer married.

Finding Light After Loss

I was functionally depressed for almost two years after my divorce, though I didn't realize it at the time. I was numb. I was not happy, but I was not sad either.

I got up and did everyday things, taking care of my children and ensuring that their needs were met, but I felt nothing, no passion for the things I used to enjoy, no dreams, no aspirations. I was literally just putting one foot in front of the other sleepwalking in a sense.

I still went to church; I attended Bahamas Harvest Church, and at the time, we had a series about living your dreams, not giving up and trying to find your passion again. We studied in small groups and in one of the meetings they asked, "So what's your dream? Where do you see yourself in five to ten years?"

And in a moment of total transparency, I said, "I don't see myself anywhere. I just see myself getting up every day, and making it happen for the children, but personally, I don't have any dreams." I thought the way I was feeling was okay because I didn't know anything different in my adulthood.

That night, the group members helped me to realize that I was mistaken. They showed me that life was meant to be lived, and that I ought to be passionate about it. Then they prayed for me to get my joy back.

After that night, I got up every morning and prayed, "God, reignite in me passion and a zeal for life. I want to be able to smile again. I want to be able to laugh again."

Society largely labels divorce as the ultimate sin from which there is no come back. However, I believe that even in divorce, God still saw me. He was still with me every step of the way, willing and able to make things happen for me and my children who are His children.

God *did* answer that prayer. It did not happen instantaneously, but it happened. I became determined that no matter what happened, I was going to make the best of it. I will be honest, I occasionally feel myself falling into that depressed state again.

Even now as I write this, I realize that its been a while since I've laughed or smiled. Life is not all that I had dreamed, and everything is not the way I envisioned it to be.

Sometimes I don't understand why I am the way that I am or why things are the way that they are, but through the questions and the resets, my resilience is at the foundation. I'm going to push past this with one foot in the front of the other; and continue to give it my all with God at the forefront.

I want everyone to know that the abundant life doesn't always relate to money as much as it does to living in every area of your life. You should be flourishing—mentally, spiritually, emotionally, and physically.

I'm not an advocate for just getting a divorce for divorce sake. Absolutely not. However, I don't think God designed it where you should stay in a loveless, abusive, dead relationship. That is not abundant living.

The most valuable lesson I learnt that I would like to share is that regardless of how it may seem, God still has His hands on us, and that He still sees us after divorce.

It may not appear that He does because of the trials and tribulations that we go through, but He has not forgotten.

I think about the story with Hagar and Ishmael in Scripture where Hagar did everything according to God's instructions, and yet, she and her son were banished from everything that they knew. That had to have been a hard pill to swallow.

As for me, I thought I did things the right way. I was a virgin until I got married. I was a Christian, not perfect, but I, as they say, *walked the walk* that God would have me to.

Yet, here I am, a divorced, single mother. I look at other women who are openly not living that straight up life, and doing everything except pleasing and serving God, but have husbands who love them, and takes care of them, some not even having to work. I used to look to God and ask *why?*

We don't always understand the way God works, and my situation was hard for me to accept. I came to the realization that not because we live the good life as God commands us to, does it guarantee a perfect life, perfect husband, perfect family, free from heartache and disappointment.

All you can do is ask God what it is He wants you to learn, and how you can still be an example for Him in whatever situation you are in. And even though it may seem as if God has forgotten you, or He doesn't see your efforts to serve Him, know that He has not forgotten you.

He still sees you, and He is still taking care of you, in the middle of everything that seems to be falling apart.

Lessons in Resilience and Grace

As my children get older, I am increasingly learning that single parenting is not for the weak. I must be both mother and father, friend and foe, loving parent and disciplinarian. It is a fine line to maneuver between and many times I feel that I am failing at it. I have no one to play good cop/bad cop with.

It is not easy to not let the anger and bitterness I feel towards their father seep through.

In weak moments I think about how he is living life without having any responsibility towards the children in any way—not spiritually, financially or emotionally—while I deal with struggles of dealing with the fallouts and gaps, day in and day out. It is so important for me to be careful and keep a prayerful heart to avoid falling into hatred towards him.

On good days, I would say God will deal with him. On bad days, I find myself saying *God it is not fair that he gets to move on while I am left to pick up the pieces.*

I am learning my triggers to falling into a negative depressive mindset. Once I find that I am dwelling on negative thoughts—things that I wish were better or how life is so unfair—I try to get busy and not focus on myself.

In 2023, following in my daughter's footsteps, I joined Kiwanis Club Fort Montagu. Kiwanis is a service organization filled with volunteers who help the less fortunate, more specifically the children of the country.

This volunteerism has caused me to focus less on what I don't have and realize that I am blessed even though it may not feel like it at times.

I know that I am the resilient woman I am because I have been blessed with a great community, and my mother, Veronica Newton, and my aunt, Laverne Sturrup, stand shoulders above them all.

I have watched my community weather death, divorce and other kinds of life's storms and come out stronger. My family is what I would call grass-root Bahamian—sons and daughters of the Bahamian soil.

My mother and aunt were great encouragers, cheerleaders, but also real-life checkers. They loved me but never let me get away with anything, not even lying to myself. They strive every day to live for Christ and push me to do the same. They hold me accountable and are there for me when life gets hard.

Daring to Dream Again

Despite all that has happened, I can dream again. I still want to have a stable family home with a loving husband. I realize it may not seem like a big goal but for me it seems almost impossible.

I am in my mid-forties, with teen-aged children. I don't know of too many men who would be interested in a situation like mine. Another dream is to do work relating to my passions of writing and editing. I also want to travel around the world with my family, exploring different cultures and food.

What Life Has Taught Me

Looking back, I see that I went into marriage naively, not realizing all that would be required to sustain a lifelong relationship. From my experience, I have learnt that in a marriage you must give it one hundred percent.

While it is a hard thing to do, own your mistakes and the missteps you took that led to the breakup, and realize that it takes two to make a marriage and two to separate.

I also learned that you should love those who love you; however, know that love is not enough. Love cannot pay bills and sustain a relationship when tough times come (and they will).

A woman is not a gold digger because she wants to ensure that the man she is committing her life to is able to sustain her financially. Marry a man who can make you laugh and shows his faithfulness, commitment, and stick-ability in other areas of his life as well. This is usually a good precursor to what life will be like with him.

As I began, I will end. Growing up, I had an ideal life, but instead of being grateful, I felt entitled, and I developed a false sense of who I was, and what life was about.

Because God loves me so much, He refused to allow me to go through life that way, so He allowed some things in my life to break me, not destroy me, and to teach me and mold me into who He wants me to be.

He is still working on me every day and I giving me a glimpse of what He has for me, and I am fully trusting that whatever it is, it is way better than anything I could have imagined because he created me, and he will complete the work in me.

As a result of my journey, I feel the motivation to expand my authorship and create small groups for single mothers to walk along side them as they navigate life and parenting. I hope this chapter encourages those women to keep God close and keep going no matter what.

I am passionate about improving myself and other women - in three areas -as a working professional, a mother and as an individual. I want to be bolder in my message regarding my divorce and issues and how I am going to help and impact other women in their journey.

Why I Am Sharing My Story

I'm sharing my story because women need to see what real strength looks like — not the kind that smiles through pain and quotes a scripture, but the kind that learns to budget, endure, and mature through it.

I want to be the woman I needed when I was balancing bills, babies, and broken promises. The woman who could look me in the eye and say, *"You're not crazy, you're growing. You're not behind, you're becoming."*

There's this quiet assumption that if you "do it right" — wait for marriage, honor God, build the house, raise the kids — the reward will be peace and stability.

But what happens when you do all that and still end up divorced, raising children alone, and staring at an empty account? What happens when you realize that holiness doesn't exempt you from hardship?

That was me. And that's why I share my story — because I had to learn how to rebuild, not from inspiration, but from necessity.

There's a kind of maturity life forces on you when you have to stretch one paycheck to cover three needs. I learned early that emotional strength means nothing if you can't be a good steward of what's in your hands.

My parents and my first boss taught me the habit that became my survival tool: *write it down, count the cost, and live by the numbers.*

Every paycheck was a map — every bill accounted for, every dollar given a destination before it had a chance to disappear. I broke big things into small things: car insurance divided by 52 weeks, school fees split by month, groceries calculated to the penny.

I didn't wait for miracles — I managed the means. That's maturity. And it's not glamorous like how you would think if you watch people on social media.

For me, it meant staying home and cooking dinner when others were going out to eat at restaurants every weekend. It meant packing lunch instead of buying it. It was watching others travel every other month while I vacationed once a year, because I knew the season I was in, and my season requires patience.

People talk about "faith" like it's magic, but faith without maturity is just wishful thinking. Faith says, *"God will provide."* Maturity says, *"And until He does, I'll plan wisely with what He's already given me."*

I had to learn deferred gratification — to wait for what I wanted, to say *not now* instead of *never.* That's something our generation doesn't celebrate enough.

Everyone wants instant results, instant comfort, instant validation. But growth requires stillness. There's beauty in sitting small for a season, knowing you won't always have to.

I learned to treat money as ministry — not an idol, not a weapon, but a tool. Stewardship became my form of worship. Because every time I honored what I had, I saw God multiply it. Every time I resisted the urge to spend carelessly, I found peace that no luxury could match.

And through it all, I grew. Not just financially, but emotionally. I learned not to fight every battle. I learned that sometimes the most powerful response is silence. That you can't control your children's choices, your ex's behavior, or life's timing — but you can control how you show up.

Maturity is knowing that your joy can't depend on anyone else's apology. That your peace is too expensive to trade for control. That everything in life has a season — and rushing one will ruin the next.

That's why I share my story. Because I want women to know that resilience is not just survival — it's stewardship, it's structure, it's self-control. It's learning to love yourself enough to stop being your own worst enemy.

I share because I've lived long enough to know that money won't fix loneliness, and love won't erase a lack of discipline. Both require wisdom. Both require waiting. Both require the kind of maturity that's built in silence and proven over time.

So this story isn't about perfection. It's about process. It's about learning to breathe through what you can't change, manage what you can, and trust God with the rest.

If you're reading this, and you're somewhere between the breakdown and the breakthrough — keep building. Keep budgeting. Keep believing. You are not failing. You are maturing.

And when the season shifts, you'll thank yourself for not rushing the lesson.

The Power of Mentorship

I believe mentorship is life's way of keeping us connected. None of us were meant to do this journey alone. Every stage I've been through — marriage, motherhood, divorce, rebuilding — has shown me the value of having women who pour into you *and* being that woman for someone else.

Mentorship doesn't always look like someone sitting across a desk giving advice. Sometimes it's a phone call from a friend who just listens. Sometimes it's an older woman at church who says, *"Trust me, you'll get through this."* And sometimes it's a simple reminder from the Holy Spirit Himself, whispering, *"You're not losing — I'm growing you."*

I've learned that "iron sharpens iron" isn't about who knows more — it's about who's willing to share what they've learned the hard way. I've made mistakes. I've stayed when I should've left. I've walked away when I was tired of fighting alone.

But every single lesson — every scar — has turned into something I can now give away.

That's what mentorship is to me. It's not about titles or platforms. It's about using your story as a bridge for someone else to cross. It's about saying, *"I've walked that road, too. Here's what helped me keep my footing."*

I want to connect with other women who have lived through the breaking and are now learning to build again. I want to share what I've learned about patience, about not rushing your healing, about how to get up and go to work even when you feel like falling apart.

I want to fill other women's cups the same way mine has been filled — by mothers, friends, coworkers, and mentors who reminded me that I still had something left to give. Even when life stripped away everything familiar, they taught me how to keep pouring — carefully, slowly, but faithfully.

And I don't just mean emotional support. I'm talking practical wisdom too — how to manage your money without losing your mind, how to budget for peace, how to say no when "yes" costs too much. Because sometimes the best mentorship doesn't sound deep — it just sounds real.

That's the kind of mentor I want to be: honest, grounded, God-led, and human. The kind of woman who tells you, *"You can cry, but don't quit."* The kind who prays with you, then reminds you to pay that bill on time.

We learn from each other's stories. We grow through shared experiences. And if my story can make another woman feel seen, steady, and a little more hopeful about her tomorrow — then everything I've walked through will have been worth it.

Seeds for Your Own Bloom

Every story plants something. Sometimes it's truth wrapped in tears. Sometimes it's wisdom born from waiting. Sometimes it's faith, tenderly rebuilt from the rubble of disappointment.

I don't share my story to dwell on what broke me — I share it so another woman can find herself in the breaking, too. I've come to understand that healing doesn't happen all at once. It happens in *seasons* — in the quiet, sometimes lonely spaces between loss and discovery.

There were times I wanted to rush the process, to skip straight to the part where everything made sense again. But God, in His mercy, slowed me down. He taught me that every season has a purpose, even the painful ones. Some seasons prune us. Others plant us. And if we stay faithful through them all, each one prepares us for the harvest ahead.

There were seasons of survival — when the goal was simply to get through the day. There were seasons of stretching — when my faith had to grow stronger than my fear. And then there were seasons of stillness — where God said, "Be patient. I'm working beneath the surface."

Those are the seasons that built me. They tested my endurance, shaped my maturity, and deepened my trust in His timing. And through it all, I learned that peace is not found in control —

it's found in surrender. These lessons became the SEEDS that shaped my becoming:

S – Support and Sisterhood

I learned that strength doesn't mean solitude. Healing happens faster when you allow others to walk beside you. There's a sacred power in sisterhood — in being seen, heard, and understood. You are not alone, and you were never meant to do this life alone.

E – Endurance in Every Season

Endurance isn't glamorous. It looks like showing up when you're exhausted. It sounds like whispered prayers when words fail. It feels like taking one small step at a time, even when you can't see where it's leading. But it's in those slow, faithful steps that God builds unshakeable strength.

E – Embrace the Truth

Divorce is not failure. It's not a label, it's a chapter — and chapters don't define the entire book. I had to unlearn the shame and remember that I am not what ended; I am what endured. Healing began the moment I stopped asking, "Why did this happen to me?" and started asking, "What is God teaching me through this?"

D – Discernment and Delay

Maturity taught me the power of patience. Not everything has to happen right now. There's grace in waiting, in saving, in planning for what's ahead. I learned to sit still when I wanted to move, to say "not yet" when everything in me screamed "go."

hing in me screamed "go." That discipline became my protection. That waiting became my wisdom.

S – Stewardship of the Soul

True healing is as practical as it is spiritual. It's managing what's in your hands — your time, your money, your peace — with reverence. I learned to build structure in the natural while trusting God in the supernatural. Stewardship became my act of worship, my way of saying, "Lord, I'm ready for more, and I'll care well for what You've already given me."

The space between the seed and the bloom is where faith matures. It's the waiting ground — the quiet middle where everything in you wants to give up, yet something holy whispers, *"Keep going."* That's where roots dig deep, where identity takes shape, and where your heart learns the rhythm of God's timing.

You cannot rush the bloom. You cannot force fruit before its season. But if you stay planted — if you endure the pruning, if you keep showing up in faith — something beautiful will rise from what once felt buried.

And when that moment comes, when the weight finally lifts and you can see light again, that's when you BLOOM.

B – Believe in Every Season

Believe that God is still working, even in silence. Some miracles don't announce themselves — they grow quietly, like roots in the dark.

L – Lean on Others

Let people pour into you. You've spent so long being the strong one, holding everything together. But true strength is knowing when to rest in someone else's faith until yours rises again.

O – Own Your Journey

Stop apologizing for your story. Every tear watered something in you. Every disappointment taught you something about discernment, discipline, and dependence on God. Own it all — the messy, the miraculous, the in-between. It's yours, and it's sacred.

O – Overcome with Grace

Grace doesn't erase what happened — it redeems it. It allows you to look back without bitterness, to move forward without fear, and to bless what once broke you.

M – Move with the Seasons, Not Against Them

Life is a cycle of sowing, growing, pruning, and blooming. Don't rush it. Don't resent it. Flow with it. Because the same God who allowed the storm also prepared the soil for your next garden.

My rose is burgundy — deep, steady, and strong. It symbolizes unwavering faith, quiet power, and beauty that endures.

Burgundy reminds me that strength doesn't have to shout. It's found in calm resilience, in grace under pressure, in the woman who keeps standing even when the world expects her to fall. There is beauty in that kind of strength — not loud or showy, but anchored, graceful, and sure.

So if my story has planted anything in you, let it be this: You are not alone. You are not a failure. And you are not finished. God is still writing your next chapter. He is still nurturing your roots in the unseen.

And when the time is right — when your faith has deepened and your endurance has done its work — you, too, will rise.

Not as who you once were, but as who you were always meant to become. Whole. Healed. And gracefully, powerfully blooming.

To my mother,

Veronica Newton

You showed me how to stay steadfast and faithful, even when the road was long and the weight was heavy.

Because of you, I learned that endurance is holy and that faith never fails.

On Eagles Wings

SHILAND A. BOSFIELD

I COULD HEAR THE fire crackling around me, its searing heat licking at my skin. My clothes were aflame, and I knew my flesh would be next. There was nothing that could be done to stop it.

As I looked up to the heavens, preparing for what seemed inevitable, something miraculous happened. I began to rise—slowly, steadily—from the flames. No hands lifted me—it was a force from within, propelling me upward.

No, that didn't actually happen. It's an allegory—a reflection of my life. Time and again, it felt like the fires of my circumstances would consume me entirely. I've been beaten down, physically and emotionally, left with no strength to stand.

And yet, by God's grace, I always rose again—emerging from the ashes like a phoenix, not just to run, but to soar! Isaiah 40:31

became my lifeline: “But those who hope in the Lord will renew their strength.

They will soar on wings like eagles; they will run and not grow weary; they will walk and not be faint.”

Like many women, I longed for love, marriage, and a family—a sense of belonging, the comfort of being wanted, needed and seen. I desired to feel beautiful, alive, and deeply loved in a healthy, thriving relationship. I sought that dream three times, and each time, it crumbled at my feet.

The First Fire

I grew up in a single-parent home surrounded by strong women. As the child of an extramarital affair, I vowed not to follow the same path.

From an early age, I knew I wanted a committed, monogamous relationship. Being the “other woman” was never an option. I knew what I didn’t want—but I had no idea how to attain what I did and still ended up in relationships that were far from ideal.

My mother strongly advised me not to get involved with my first husband. But did I listen? No. I dated him anyway and this decision strained my relationship with her, but I was in love...or so I thought. I believed I was grown enough to understand what love and marriage were all about.

In the beginning, things were good. He was attentive, affectionate, and seemed content to stay home with me rather than go out with friends. We were happy.

Then the shift began. He started staying out for hours, almost daily. We had a toddler son by then. He would pick him up from preschool, drop him home, and leave again without explanation.

That slow unraveling was, as the saying goes, the beginning of the end.

Despite his own frequent absences, he accused me of having an affair. One evening, his accusations turned violent. He attacked me as our little boy stood helpless in the doorway, crying and begging his father to stop. It was a harrowing experience.

The police were called. I was taken to the hospital for evaluation, and that night, I left both the apartment and the marriage. Around midnight, I was driven away in a police vehicle, leaving my two-year-old son with his father.

I spent the night in the hospital and was discharged around 5 a.m. With no relationship with my family at the time, I had nowhere to go.

However, a friend took me in — despite already sharing her small two-bedroom apartment with her boyfriend, four children, and a grandchild. She squeezed me in anyway.

The next day, I returned with police assistance and regained custody of my son. We shared a double bed with my friend. She did her best to make us feel welcome, despite the chaos.

Looking back, I know I could've turned to my mother, but I was too stubborn, too proud. I had a point to prove—I was capable of doing life on my own. I didn't want to hear "I told you so." The relationship between my family and I was already too strained for that.

Weeks later, my mother heard about the breakup and reached out. She asked me to come home. I was just 25 years old, and I had already lived through a life-altering, traumatic experience. My mother died never knowing the full story of what happened that night.

Back at home, trying to rebuild, I discovered my ex-husband was watching me. He would call or send messages detailing my exact location, clothing, and companions. I later learned he was either following me himself or having friends spy on me. I was terrified.

In desperation, I moved to a different island, hoping to escape. But even there, the harassment continued. Detailed messages arrived—what I was wearing, where I'd been, and who I was with.

The fear was unbearable. Why was he doing this? Was he hoping for reconciliation? Or simply trying to make my life miserable? Whatever his motives, he failed. Instead of making me crumble, his actions ignited a fierce determination within me.

I refused to stay stuck in the pain and disappointment. I filed for divorce, and in 2008—five years after our separation—my first divorce was finalized.

When the marriage ended, I felt defeated. Inadequacy crept in. My idea of marriage had not survived reality. But even then, I clung to hope. Somewhere out there, I believed, was the love I had always dreamed of—the partner I was meant for, still searching for me.

The Second Fire

I met my second husband in 2006, while still legally married to my first. We crossed paths on one of the family islands.

At the time, he was entangled in a turbulent relationship, and I was supposedly healing from mine.

We shared heart-to-heart conversations—his about a dysfunctional present, mine about a broken past. We bonded through pain, which I later realized was trauma bonding.

He seemed like a victim, and that awoke something in me: my superhero complex. I stepped into the role without hesitation. In my mind, love could fix anything, even deep emotional wounds.

Within months, we talked about moving in together, having a child, and even marriage. I ignored the red flags. I silenced every warning whisper in my soul.

I believed that with enough love, everything would fall into place.

And for a brief time, it did. In 2008, we welcomed a baby girl. She was our joy, a fresh beginning. But the joy was short-lived.

One night, while she was still under a year old, we had a fierce argument.

It escalated quickly. He pinned me to the bed and threatened to harm me—even as I held our baby in my arms. He showed no concern for her safety, or mine.

When he finally let go, he ripped her from my arms and stormed out, taking her with him. He didn't return that night, nor did he answer my frantic calls.

Once again, I had to call the police to regain custody of my child. He disappeared, leaving the island without a trace or any hint of return. That incident should have been enough.

It should have been my moment of clarity—the déjà vu of another abusive cycle. But I was still clinging to the hope of love, the idea that someone out there could share my dreams, heal my wounds, and stay.

What sustained me during that season were the acts of kindness from friends and colleagues—vessels of God's mercy in my life. When he left, he took his car, leaving me and our infant daughter stranded.

A colleague from my department offered me her vehicle. She brought it to me every morning so I could take my daughter to daycare. That simple act of generosity etched itself into my heart forever.

I wasn't a Christian yet, but I started to recognize the patterns. The lifelines God kept sending. The subtle rescues, the unexplainable provisions.

My heart was searching for something—something I couldn't name. Something just beyond my reach. Something I knew I needed.

Eventually, I realized what it was. It wasn't just help or healing—it was Him. I opened my heart to Jesus Christ and accepted Him as my Lord and Savior.

But this wasn't the conclusion of my story. It was only the beginning of a new chapter. Not long after, my daughter's father returned. And yes—we rekindled the relationship.

In May 2009, he proposed to me in church, in front of the entire congregation. It felt redemptive, hopeful. For a short while, we were happy. But less than two months after our wedding, I lost my job.

Days later, I found out I was pregnant again. By then, we were struggling. I was unemployed, he was self-employed, and we had two babies—one just two years old, the other barely six months. We had to turn to the Department of Social Services just to afford basic baby necessities.

Then came what looked like a breakthrough—a job offer on one of the Exuma Cays. The pay was good—$600 a week—and I believed it was God's provision. But what happened after could only be described as spiritual warfare.

The job separated us. I went to Exuma, my husband stayed in Nassau, and our daughters were sent to live with his mother in Andros. Leaving my kids was painful, but I told myself it was temporary...that I was doing it for them—for their future.

But a few months in, things fell apart again. My husband and I had a heated argument over the phone. He threatened to take my daughters and keep them from me forever.

It was happening again. The fear. The panic. The heartbreak. My second marriage was unravelling before my eyes.

Still, God strengthened me once more. He brought the right people at the right time—just as He always had. A fellow church member, a female police sergeant stationed on the Exuma mainland, took my case to heart.

It wasn't luck that she was on duty that day—it was divine timing. She helped me coordinate with social services and the local police in both Exuma and Mangrove Cay.

The plan was precise: I would fly to Nassau, stay overnight, then travel with my mother to Mangrove Cay the next morning. Together, we would collect my daughters and return to Nassau that same day.

By this time, my mother and I had fully reconciled. She stood by me through it all. I had just enough money in my account to cover the entire journey. Every detail worked out. Every step made possible. And just like that—I was reunited with my daughters.

Once again, I found myself single. But this time, I had three small children: a ten-year-old, a toddler, and an infant. It was not the life I envisioned, but by God's grace, we survived.

In truth, I had already been carrying the weight alone. My husband had done very little to support our children during our time together.

Now, alone again, I was rebuilding. And despite the heartbreak of two failed marriages, I remained a romantic at heart. I still believed love was out there. And soon, I would meet husband number three.

The Final Blow

We met in 2013, and from the beginning, I truly believed he was the one God had kept just for me. I poured my heart out to my suitor, he knew everything I had endured. I thought this relationship would redeem all the heartache and disappointments of the past. I was smitten—and blinded.

There were signs I should have noticed, things that should have made me pause. When we met, he was still married to his first wife. But according to him, it was over. They were no longer living together. I wanted so much to believe him.

He painted every woman from his past as a villain—unfaithful, manipulative, unappreciative. In every story, he was the victim. And I believed every word. My superhero complex kicked in again.

I saw myself as the one who could bring healing, stability, and love. I was ready to build something new, something real. We got married in February 2017.

At first, it seemed promising, but everything changed after I was diagnosed with Multiple Sclerosis. My health began to decline, and so did our marriage. What I thought was love and partnership began to unravel.

The person I had trusted with my life became unrecognizable. Then, in June of 2023, my world collapsed when he confessed to having a one-year-old daughter from an affair within our marriage.

I had already suspected something. That intuitive feeling wouldn't leave me, so I asked, and the truth came out.

But what followed was even more heartbreaking: he asked me to sign legal documents acknowledging his illegitimate child. There was no remorse, no apology—just a cruel request that felt like another betrayal layered on top of many others.

That wasn't the end. He began maneuvering to take control of the home I had fought so hard to build for my children and myself.

Over the years his financial contribution in the day-to-day maintenance of the home we shared had been minimal, but now he wanted authority over everything. I felt used, deceived and discarded.

As I sat replaying the events of our marriage, a chilling realization settled over me: I didn't truly know the man I had vowed my life to. There was no remorse in him, no hint of regret, no willingness to take accountability.

Our marriage wasn't perfect—no marriage is—and I had my own shortcomings, difficult as they were to admit and address. But instead of acknowledging his choices, he placed the blame for his infidelity on me, refusing to accept responsibility for any part of what had unfolded.

It became clear: closure would never come from him. So, I sought it from the only Source I could trust—my Lord and Savior. He had carried me before, and He would carry me now.

The final divorce was granted in December 2024—just one day after my birthday. It was the end of another chapter, and the beginning of something else entirely.

The Mirror and the Mask

It wasn't until after my third failed marriage that I finally stopped running and began looking inward. Therapy became my lifeline. And through that process, I uncovered a truth that both broke and freed me: my choices in partners had been shaped by an unhealed wound—rejection.

The absence of my father cast a long shadow over my life. For years, I carried that invisible weight, unaware of how deeply it had affected my sense of worth. I had been trying to prove something—to someone, to everyone, to myself. I just wanted to be loved.

I believed if I gave enough, sacrificed enough, endured enough, I would earn the love I had always longed for.

It took two therapists and months of painful introspection to help me connect the dots. I had developed a pattern: I was attracted to wounded men, and once I heard their story, I would slip into my role—the savior.

With every new relationship, I thought, *"I can help. I can fix this. I'll love them whole."* I became "Shiland to the rescue," always ready to throw on my invisible cape. And for a time, it felt fulfilling. In the beginning, I was happy. I felt needed. I felt worthy.

But then the reality would set in. The red flags I had ignored at first would become impossible to deny. The emotional distance, the manipulation, the broken promises.

The boundaries—if they ever existed—would slowly erode, either pushed aside by them or neglected by me. By then, I was too invested—emotionally, physically, financially. I didn't want to start over. I was terrified of more rejection. That fear kept me trapped.

The hardest truth to accept was that there were common threads woven through all of my relationships. Each of these men carried unresolved trauma. And so did I. The difference was, I kept trying to heal others while bleeding myself.

But here's what I now know: there is nothing shameful about having trauma. The danger lies in ignoring it, denying it, or pretending it doesn't affect our choices.

I had to literally look up the definition of trauma. One stood out: "An experience that produces psychological injury or pain."

That definition unlocked everything. I realized so many of us go through life unaware that we're walking around wounded—and unintentionally wounding others in the process.

After my third marriage ended, I struggled with depression. There were days when the weight was so heavy, even the smallest harsh word could make me burst into tears.

I lost time—blocks of memory simply gone. But I kept it all inside. I smiled when I wanted to scream. I looked polished when I felt broken.

We attended the same church, my ex and I. So, every Sunday became a performance. I put on my best outfit and a radiant smile, determined to look better than I felt.

People wondered how I stayed so composed. Sometimes, I wondered too. But every time I saw his car in the parking lot; it was like someone ripped the Band-Aid off a barely healing wound. Still, I wouldn't let anyone—especially him—see me suffer.

By the time we met, I was a Christian, but I wasn't spiritually mature. With my first two husbands, I wasn't walking with Christ at all.

But if I had been stronger in my faith when I met my third husband, I would have had the courage to say, *"This relationship does not align with my values, and it does not meet my needs."* I regret not saying it then. But I thank God, I can say it now without any further regret.

All of it—the trauma, the therapy, the heartbreak—taught me a powerful truth: even when I couldn't trace God's hand, He was still there, working it all together for my good.

Adversity to Triumph

Looking back on all three marriages, I can honestly say—I am not the woman I once was. Each relationship brought its own set of hardships, yet I entered every marriage with renewed hope.

I refused to let the pain of one experience close me off to the possibility of love in the next. Somehow, there was always a resilience deep within me—a strength I couldn't always explain at the time.

I didn't fully understand what kept me going; I just knew I had to keep moving forward.

Now I know: it wasn't *what* kept me—it was *Who*. God never let me go. He used each heartbreak, every fire, to shape and refine me. The woman I am today was forged in those flames.

I'm now on a genuine journey of self-discovery. I'm learning to see the red flags I once ignored, to recognize my own emotional patterns, and to identify what truly matters to me.

It wouldn't be fair to say I'm rediscovering myself—because truthfully, I don't think I ever truly knew who "Shiland" was. For most of my life, I did things to please others, craving their validation and approval.

Now, I'm learning to be comfortable in my own skin. If love finds me again, it must be sent by God—and it must meet me in the fullness of who I am. I no longer accept love that requires me to shrink, settle, or lose myself.

I've come to realize that when a man truly loves a woman, there is nothing he wouldn't do to cherish and support her.

I saw this firsthand during routine appointments with my neurologist in the United States. I watched husbands push their wives in wheelchairs. I saw wives holding their husbands' hands in waiting rooms.

Those quiet, powerful moments made something click inside me: my marriages didn't fail because I wasn't good enough, or because I wasn't meant for love. They failed because *we weren't meant for each other*.

For years, I made decisions that prioritized the happiness of others—many times at the expense of my own well-being. I thought I was being loving. In truth, I was being self-sacrificing in unhealthy ways.

I put others on pedestals, believing they saw me the same way. But when it mattered most, I was left unsupported and alone.

This wasn't only in my three failed marriages but in some friendships as well.

In each of my marriages, I surrendered pieces of myself—my dreams of traveling, time with friends and family—just to create peace. I thought boundaries were optional. I didn't understand their value until my third marriage collapsed. Then, the lesson hit me like a beam of light. Boundaries are not selfish; they are necessary.

Yes, I've been hurt. Some of that pain I invited, some I didn't. But through it all, I refused to become bitter. I prayed that God would keep my heart soft. I asked Him to take the broken pieces and shape them into something beautiful. And He has.

I can say, with confidence and pride, that every heartbreak I endured helped reinvent my heart—not to make it harder, but to make it wiser, stronger, more compassionate. I am now a woman walking fully in God's grace.

Healing the Roots

I still have fears. Some, I've overcome through God's grace. Others, I continue to place in His hands, one prayer at a time. One of my deepest fears was forming a relationship with my biological father.

For most of my life, I worried that if I reached out, he would reject me again. But after my third marriage ended—and through the continued help of therapy—I finally found the courage to try.

To my surprise, he responded. He now visits me and my daughters, checks in with us, and shows up in a way I never imagined he would. His presence has helped me realize just how deeply I had yearned for a father figure all along.

Another fear I carried was that I wouldn't be able to provide for or nurture my children. I wanted so badly to be for them what my mother was for me and my sister: a pillar of strength, and a steady presence they could always count on.

My mother wasn't openly affectionate, but we never questioned her love. Not once. Her love language was a quiet, practical devotion—the kind that holds everything together when it feels like everything is falling apart. I now see that strength in myself.

Still, I have moments when I feel like I'm failing—especially after my last marriage ended, and my relationship with my son became strained. Those feelings creep in, whispering that I'm not doing enough, but I've learned to turn those whispers over to the Lord. His guidance, comfort, and provision carry me through.

Motherhood hasn't been easy, but it has been sacred. I've walked through the fire and come out with a deeper love for my children and a clearer understanding of the mother I want to be.

From early on, I dreamed of owning a home. Before the birth of my first child, I was already working toward that goal. Life had other plans—setbacks, disappointments, and detours.

Giving up was never an option. I kept going, step by step, sometimes crawling, but always moving forward.

And now, after three failed marriages and years of struggle, my daughters and I are finally living in a home we can call our own. Not just a roof over our heads, but a space built through perseverance, prayer, and the unshakeable grace of God.

Resilience in Women

While I hope my story inspires you, I want you to understand this: my resilience did not just appear. It runs in my blood. I come from a lineage of strong, enduring women—my grandmother, my mother, and my sister—each one a pillar in her own right.

My grandmother suffered deeply in her marriage. She was physically abused by her husband, who often took the little money she earned from her secret jobs. Despite the violence, despite discovering he had another family, she carried on.

When he finally left, she was left to raise their two young children—my mom and uncle—entirely on her own. She took jobs as a domestic worker, and when her employers gave her meals during the day, she didn't eat them. She carefully packed them away and brought them home for her children.

That was the kind of woman she was—selfless, resourceful, and quietly heroic. My mother, too, knew disappointment. Her attempt at marriage ended quickly when her husband left shortly after the wedding.

The marriage was annulled, and she found herself a single mother of two young girls. With only my grandmother by her side, she raised us the best way she knew how.

Things were tough for a long time. But she never gave up. She didn't quit. Eventually, with the help of my older sister—who started working early to support us—my mother was able to buy a home of her own. She faced her share of hardships, but she stood tall until the very end, passing away in 2017 with dignity and strength.

My sister has walked her own difficult road as well, but like the women before her, she held it together and pressed on. She retired at sixty, a testament to perseverance and focus.

When I look at my lineage, I understand something very clearly: Resilience is not optional for me. It's who I am. It's what I know. It's what I inherited.

Moving Forward

The Lord has been my strength through every storm. He is the reason I am still standing. His grace has sustained me through heartbreak, hardship, and healing. He was there through every relationship, every trial, every quiet cry behind closed doors. And now, I see it clearly—God doesn't waste anything—not even our pain.

Each test, each valley, each tear has served a purpose. They shaped me, prepared me, and are now being used for His glory. One of the most powerful reminders of this truth came during a zip-lining trip in El Salvador. I was terrified.

I had made it to the first tightrope, but fear paralyzed me. I refused to move. Then, a young female attendant walked the tightrope toward me. She clipped her carabiner to my harness, gently took my hand, and walked me across.

That was all I needed. Just one person to walk me through the first step. After that, I crossed the rest of the tightropes on my own. She taught me how to move forward: one foot in front of the other, heel to toe. Step by step.

That's how healing works. That's how faith works. God has given me a forgiving heart—not to excuse the harm others have caused, but to free me from being bound to it. Bitterness steals too much. Forgiveness, on the other hand, liberates and it does not mean reconciliation or continued access.

Because I am a child of God and they are too, if they were in true need and the Holy Spirit instructs me to help them, I will. That's not weakness—that's God's strength in me.

As a believer, I know that when I sin and repent, my Heavenly Father forgives me. The Bible tells us that no sin is greater than another. So if God, in His holiness, forgives others—who am I to withhold that same grace? That's why I choose forgiveness. Not because it's easy, but because it's necessary for peace and progress.

Soaring On

Today, I walk with renewed strength, boldness, and determination. I'm no longer surviving—I'm soaring. Let me say this clearly: resilience isn't something you're born with—it's something you grow into. It's a mindset. A choice. And if I can develop it, so can you.

There's so much I missed while trying to hold everything together. So many dreams I deferred. But now, I'm catching up on life. I'm traveling. I'm laughing more. I'm allowing myself to experience new places, people, food, and cultures. And with every step, I feel more alive—more like the woman I was always meant to be.

I've faced life's challenges, and I know the weight of pain, but I've also discovered the power of healing. I want to walk alongside others, guiding them to uncover their self-worth, confidence, and inner strength.

Through compassionate mentorship grounded in empathy and understanding, I want to help women transform struggles into growth and pain into power, empowering them to embrace their true potential.

Why I Am Sharing My Story

There was a time when silence felt safer than honesty. I smiled through heartbreak, laughed through loneliness, and convinced myself that strength meant surviving quietly. But the truth is—silence may protect your pride, yet it strangles your healing. My story begins the moment I chose to speak.

For years, I carried the weight of rejection, disappointment, and illness like heavy luggage I was too afraid to unpack. I thought I was protecting myself, but in reality, I was protecting my pain.

It wasn't until I surrendered the illusion of control that God began turning what was once unbearable into something purposeful.

The heartbreaks that once defined me became blueprints for growth. The tears that once blurred my vision became water for new seeds of compassion. Through His guidance, I learned that pain isn't punishment—it's preparation. It's God's way of reshaping our hearts so that our purpose can finally fit.

When I finally started sharing my experiences—openly, honestly, without filters—I saw how powerful transparency can be. Every time I spoke, someone else exhaled. They'd whisper, "I thought I was the only one."

And that's when it clicked: this isn't just *my* story—it's *our* story. It belongs to every woman who's smiled while breaking inside, every man who's prayed for strength in the middle of the storm, every soul who's been through loss, illness, or betrayal and wondered, *Does God still see me?*

I share because I want others to know they are not alone. I share because silence breeds shame, and shame keeps too many of us stuck in cycles we were born to break. My story is a reminder that vulnerability is not weakness—it's warfare. When we speak our truth, we strip the enemy of the power to use it against us.

Resilience didn't come naturally; it was built one decision at a time. There were days I felt invisible, days when my body ached from illness and my heart from disappointment. But God's voice became my constant companion: *Get up anyway.*

And I did—again and again. I discovered that resilience isn't about bouncing back quickly; it's about believing that even when life has knocked you flat, there's still holy ground beneath your feet. I learned to rise slower, wiser, and with purpose.

My story is also a testimony of healing—a journey of rediscovering my worth in the very places I once lost it. Healing didn't just happen in prayer; it happened in practice. It happened in therapy, in long journaling sessions, in quiet walks where I learned to hear my own thoughts again.

It happened when I realized that faith and effort are partners, not opposites. You can pray for peace and still need counseling. You can believe in miracles and still have to do the work.

Every chapter of my life—the rejection, the heartbreak, the chronic illness—became a curriculum in empathy. They taught me how to see others, not through judgment, but through grace.

That's why my heart now beats for mentorship, for walking alongside others who are still navigating their own wilderness. I don't just want to tell people that healing is possible—I want to *show* them.

Through coaching, through small groups, through one-on-one conversations, my goal is to help others turn their pain into purpose, just as God helped me do.

Owning my story is how I reclaimed my power. For too long, I allowed my pain to speak louder than my progress. But now, I write and speak from a place of peace, knowing that I am not defined by what broke me—but by *Who* rebuilt me.

When I share, I'm not seeking validation. I'm planting a legacy. My words are seeds for someone else's hope, reminders that even in brokenness, beauty can still bloom.

And maybe, years from now, a woman will read these words on a day she feels like giving up. Maybe she'll see herself in my story and realize that she, too, can rise from the rubble.

That's what storytelling does—it bridges generations of faith and reminds us that no wound is wasted when it's placed in God's hands.

So I share not out of pride, but out of purpose. I share because my scars are not shameful—they are evidence! I share because my life, in all its bruised and beautiful complexity, has become living proof that there is indeed life after loss, healing after heartbreak, and joy after pain.

This is my truth, my offering, and my prayer: That every word I write becomes a spark of courage in someone else's darkness—and that through our shared stories, we all remember that even when life breaks us, God still has a plan to make us whole again.

The Power of Mentorship

Through it all, I've learned that mentorship isn't just something you do — it's something you live. It's the way your scars start to speak when words fall short, the way your story becomes a map for someone else's survival.

Every season of my life, whether filled with pain or peace, has been a classroom, and every lesson learned has turned me into both a student and a teacher.

The power of my mentorship was forged in the very places that once tried to break me. An absentee father taught me how to find my identity in God alone — not in approval, not in attention, but in divine acceptance.

The empty chair at my childhood table became the first pulpit where I learned the language of self-worth. Three marriages, each ending in heartbreak, revealed that love without alignment is not peace, and that healing begins not when someone chooses you — but when you finally choose yourself.

Those endings, as painful as they were, taught me how to stand up after collapse, how to rebuild without resentment, and how to recognize red flags from a healed heart instead of a hurting one.

Motherhood then became my mirror. Raising my children alone, I discovered that strength isn't about doing everything perfectly — it's about showing up faithfully.

Every bedtime prayer whispered through exhaustion, every tear wiped while holding back my own, became a sermon in resilience. My children didn't just teach me responsibility —

they taught me unconditional love, grace, and the truth that legacy is built not on perfection, but on presence.

When my health failed, I thought my purpose might too. Living with an autoimmune disease stripped me of energy, predictability, and at times, hope. But in that weakness, I encountered God's strength.

I learned that purpose doesn't pause for pain — it often grows inside it. Each flare-up became an invitation to lean deeper into grace, to slow down enough to hear God whisper, *You can still rise.*

Financially, I've walked through both drought and overflow. I've seen what happens when you trust God with your little and learn to steward it well. There were seasons where the math didn't add up, but His mercy did.

I worked through the exhaustion of long shifts, juggling motherhood and illness, showing up even when I had every reason to stop. I learned to plan, to save, to prepare — because faith doesn't cancel responsibility; it strengthens it.

Working my way through the pandemic; when the world shut down, I showed up. When others were shrinking back in fear, I pressed forward in faith.

Those endless hours, those aching days, those quiet prayers in the middle of exhaustion — that's where I accumulated the down payment for my home and built my confidence.

God honored that season. What felt like survival became a foundation for stability, and that blessing became my testimony of "faith plus works."

Now, as I look back, I see that mentorship isn't about perfection or position. It's about posture — the willingness to sit with someone in their pain, not to fix it, but to show them that healing is possible.

My mentorship isn't from textbooks or titles; it's from trenches. It's from surviving what was meant to destroy me and using those very experiences to strengthen others.

Every time I speak to a woman who feels unseen, or a man who's trying to rebuild after loss, I see my reflection in their eyes. And in those moments, I remember: this is what all the pain was for. To teach me how to lead with empathy. To show me that my testimony could be a torch for someone else's path.

Today, whether I'm mentoring one-on-one, serving as a life coach in the making, or simply sharing my story over coffee, I carry this truth: God never wastes a wound. Every trial was training. Every heartbreak was preparation. Every breakthrough was proof.

So when I mentor now, I don't just teach people how to survive — I teach them how to soar. Because if God could raise me from the ashes of illness, heartbreak, and disappointment, then surely He can lift them too.

Like the phoenix, I've learned to rise again and again — not with bitterness, but with wisdom. And when I extend my hand to help another woman stand, I do so as one who knows, you don't have to have it all together to be used by God. You just have to be willing to let Him use all that you've been through.

Rising on Eagle's Wings

Every story plants something — sometimes pain, sometimes strength, sometimes faith. My prayer is that as you've read mine, a seed has been planted in you — a quiet knowing that even when everything feels broken, God is still working beneath the surface.

The seeds I've sown in these pages were not planted in perfect soil. They were planted in disappointment, watered with tears, and tended through long seasons where I couldn't see a single sign of growth.

I've known what it feels like to pray for something and watch it fall apart instead. I've known the ache of working until my body gave out, the fatigue of holding a smile when my soul felt crushed, and the silence of waiting for God when I didn't know if He was even listening.

But here's what I've learned: nothing that dies in faith stays buried forever. Every buried dream, every unanswered prayer, every season of stillness was God's way of preparing me, not punishing me. Just as a seed must break to sprout, I had to be broken open to bloom.

I think often of the eagle, the very image Isaiah used to describe renewal. When an eagle ages, it doesn't die—it retreats to the mountain, shedding old feathers, breaking off its own beak, waiting in painful isolation for new strength to emerge.

It's not pretty, but it's powerful. That's what my process looked like—hidden, hard, holy. And just like that eagle, when my renewal finally came, I didn't just fly again—I soared higher than before.

So these are the SEEDS I want to leave with you. They are truths that took root in me when everything else felt uncertain—truths that grew through rejection, divorce, illness, and exhaustion, and still bloomed into purpose.

S – Surrender

Healing begins when you release your grip on how you thought it should go. I spent years trying to control outcomes—relationships, timelines, even God's plan. Surrendering didn't come easy. But when I finally laid everything down, peace met me in the ashes. Surrender wasn't defeat; it was deliverance.

E – Endurance

Faith doesn't mean you won't get tired; it means you'll keep showing up even when you are. I worked 21 days straight after the pandemic when the world was still reeling. My feet hurt, my body ached, but every shift, every late night, every exhausted prayer was an act of faith. That endurance became the bridge to my breakthrough.

E – Empowerment

Power doesn't come from pretending you're strong. It comes from letting God's strength rise in your weakness. I used to think empowerment meant independence—until God showed me it's about dependence on Him. Every scar became a source of wisdom, every failure a lesson in strength.

D – Divine Direction

When everything was falling apart, God was still drawing a map. What felt like detours were really directions—each heartbreak, each disappointment leading me exactly where I was meant to be. I stopped fighting the redirections and started following the whispers.

S – Stewardship

What I've lived through isn't just for me. The blessings I've been given, the healing I've experienced, even the wisdom I've gained—these are not trophies; they're tools. Stewardship means managing your miracles well, turning lessons into legacy.

The Space Between the Seed and the Bloom

The hardest part of any transformation is the in-between. That silent, stretching space where nothing seems to be happening. Where your faith feels tested and your heart questions if it's even worth it. That was my middle place.

Between what I planted and what I prayed for, God taught me patience. Between heartbreak and healing, He taught me hope. Between exhaustion and renewal, He taught me endurance.

I learned that the middle is where faith matures. It's where you stop needing proof and start trusting process. It's the place where God buries your old self so the new you can take root.

If you're in that space right now—if you're tired, unsure, or silently waiting—know this: growth is still happening. Roots are forming. Wings are being built in the dark. The silence isn't punishment; it's preparation. Stay in the soil. Don't dig up what you planted just because it's taking time.

Because when the time is right, you'll bloom—and you'll understand why the wait was holy.

B – Bclicvc Again

Faith begins where certainty ends. Even when life feels impossible, dare to believe again.

L – Lean on God's Strength

When you are weary, He renews. When you are empty, He fills. Let His power carry you when your own runs out.

O – Open Your Heart to Healing

Forgive. Release. Breathe. Healing is not about forgetting what happened—it's about no longer being defined by it.

O – Own Your Story

Don't hide the chapters that hurt. They are the proof of your becoming. Own them, honor them, and let them remind you how far you've come.

M – Move Forward in Faith

Faith without movement is just memory. Take the next

step—whatever it is—and trust that God's already prepared the ground beneath you.

Magenta—the color of my rose—symbolizes compassion and balance. It reminds me that strength and softness can coexist, that healing and power are not opposites but partners. It's the color of a woman who has walked through the fire and emerged refined, not ruined.

So if my story has planted anything in you, let it be this: God renews strength in seasons of weakness. Your pain has purpose. Faith will anchor you through every storm. And healing—real, lasting healing—comes when you finally surrender control and trust His timing.

This is your invitation to rise—to step into your next chapter, to walk with faith, to breathe again, and to remember that nothing about your story is wasted.

Plant your seed. Protect your soil. And when your time comes, don't just grow— Soar. On wings like eagles. From heartbreak to healing — I'm living proof that God makes beauty from brokenness.

To my mother,

Olive Queen Mitchell

You opened the doors to your home
and also your heart when the storms of
my life raged the hardest.

Because of you, I am able to stand tall in
any storm and soar on wings of grace.

Conclusion

EVERY WOMAN WHO BRAVELY said YES to the call to share her story in *Roses in Bloom* began from the soil of a painful divorce, but what you've just finished isn't a story of suffering; it's a story of becoming.

These are women who planted in faith, watered with tears, and waited through long, silent seasons — only to discover that even buried things can breathe again. Their lives prove that God does His best work in the dark: not merely reviving what was lost, but revealing what was always meant to grow.

So as you close these pages, I pray you didn't just *read* our stories — I pray you *saw yourself* in them. I pray that somewhere between these lines, you caught a glimpse of your own reflection rising, whether you are going through a divorce, a loss, a disappointment, or a hard season that feels like it will never end.

This anthology is more than a collection of testimonies. It's a blueprint for rebuilding — spiritually, emotionally, financially, and relationally. It's written for the woman standing in her "in-between," still tending her soil, wondering if anything beautiful can grow from what she's lost. It's for the one who knows that faith is not passive — it's participation. That prayer and planning can coexist. That waiting and working are both forms of worship.

Because blooming doesn't stop when the book closes. It begins the moment you decide to rise.

Each woman in these pages faced her own storm — the sting of rejection, the ache of divorce, the strain of single motherhood, the quiet fight to stand strong when everything inside was trembling. They endured heartbreaks, health battles, and financial mountains that seemed impossible to climb. And yet, every single one of them kept showing up. They kept believing. They kept blooming.

This book isn't about perfection; it's about persistence — the everyday miracle of endurance and the faith it takes to bloom in real time, under real pressure. It's about women who refused to quit, who prayed when they had no strength left, who built without a blueprint, and who trusted that even wilted flowers can bloom again.

The Process of Blooming

Blooming doesn't happen in isolation. It happens in community.

Every flower needs sunlight, but it also needs a gardener—someone to prune, to water, to protect it from the elements. That's why every woman in this anthology chose to include a special thank you at the end of her story: a space to honor the "gardeners" in her life—the mothers, pastors, mentors, friends, and spiritual sisters who watered her faith when she was weary.

For us, that community began at Bahamas Harvest Church, under the leadership of Pastors Mario & Erika Moxey, whose openness to say yes to a divorce recovery small group became sacred soil for healing. It was there that laughter returned, hearts were mended, and the seed for this very book was planted. Out of that soil came a sisterhood, each woman a rose, each story a bloom, and each chapter a testimony that nothing God plants will die before it fulfills its purpose.

If there's one thing I've learned through all of this, it's that *no woman blooms alone.* Mentorship matters. Community matters. Faith matters. So, before you move on from these pages, ask yourself: who is watering your soul? Who's helping you grow? And who are you called to nurture next? Because the moment you help another woman rise—you bloom again.

The Seeds You Must Plant

Every garden begins with a seed, and every transformation begins with a decision. The women in these pages didn't wake up healed—they *chose* to be. They didn't wake up whole—they *worked* to be. And like them, your next chapter begins when you decide to plant the right SEEDS:

S – Surrender to the Season

Stop fighting the soil you're planted in. You don't have to understand everything—just trust that God is working beneath the surface. True growth begins where your control ends.

E – Endure with Expectation

Patience is not passive. Endurance is not weakness. When life feels silent, believe that God is setting the stage for your next reveal. Stay faithful in the waiting—harvest always comes to those who don't quit.

E – Embrace Mentorship and Community

Isolation kills growth. Seek out women who challenge your mindset, nurture your spirit, and call you higher. Be teachable. Be transparent. Let iron sharpen iron.

D – Discipline and Diligence

Faith without structure is chaos. Start the business plan. Create the budget. Save when it's hard. Steward what's in your hand, and God will multiply what's in your heart.

S – Submit to God's Timing

You can't rush what Heaven is preparing. Every delay is divine redirection. Rest in the truth that your bloom will come—right on time, not before, not after.

The Bloom That Follows

Once the seeds are planted, you must protect your growth. You'll still face storms, criticism, dry seasons, and doubts. But this is where your BLOOM begins:

B – Believe Beyond What You See

Faith means looking at barren ground and still expecting a garden. Keep believing that better is coming, even when you can't see a single petal yet.

L – Let Go and Let God Lead

Release the need to figure everything out. You don't have to carry the weight of your healing or your future alone. Surrender the blueprint and let Him build it better.

O – Open Your Heart Again

To love, to purpose, to life itself. Don't let heartbreak make you hard. Soft hearts hear God's whispers. Stay open to divine surprises.

O – Obey When It's Uncomfortable

Obedience will always cost you something—time, comfort, pride—but it will never cost you purpose. Say yes to God, even when the "how" doesn't make sense.

M – Move Forward Fearlessly

The past was the classroom, not the cage. Walk boldly into your next season. Start again. Build again. Love again. You've survived enough to know that you were built to bloom.

The Garden Ahead

So, what happens after you finish reading *Roses in Bloom*? You live it.

You take the lessons of these women—Lynneka's healing, Lisa's wisdom, Shiland's resilience, Raquel's endurance, Anisia's faith, and my obedience and renewal, and you plant them in your own life. You become the next gardener, the next mentor, the next story in bloom. You lift another woman as you rise. You build legacy with your lessons.

And when your next storm comes—and it will—you remember that flowers only bloom after rain.

Because this is what *Roses in Bloom* is all about. It's not about looking perfect. It's about being planted. It's about trusting the pruning. It's about knowing that grace grows in every season, even the ones that hurt.

So, to the woman holding this book—if your petals are falling, if your soil feels dry, if your faith feels tired—don't give up.

You're not dying. You're developing.

Keep planting. Keep praying.

Keep becoming.

You are not forgotten. You are being formed.

And when your time comes—and it will—you won't just stand tall. You'll stand radiant.

Rooted. Restored.

READY.

Because the gardener never abandons what He plants.

And you, dear woman, were made to bloom.

GOD'S WORD

Roses Rooted In The Word

THIS SECTION WAS CREATED for one simple reason: every author in this anthology has a real relationship with the Word, and there were specific scriptures that carried her through the hardest seasons of her life. Each contributor chose two verses, one for her Seed season and one for her Bloom. The Seed scripture reflects the moments that were tough, unclear, or stretching. The Bloom scripture reflects the moment when things began to open up again, when clarity returned, or when she felt herself stepping into something new.

This part of the book is not here to repeat their stories. You have already walked through their journeys in full. What comes next is simply another layer of their offering, another part of the rose they are giving you. Along with their scriptures and insights, each author selected a title for her page that reflects who God proved Himself to be in her Seed season and who He revealed

Himself to be in her Bloom. These names are not labels. They are lived experiences of God's character in motion.

These reflections are intentionally simple. They are not in-depth Bible studies and they are not meant to impress. They are short and honest explanations of why a certain scripture mattered at a specific time. You will see what was happening for them personally, how that scripture held them steady, and what they hope someone else might draw from it. It is meaningful because behind every verse is an author who lived through something real and trusted God to guide her in the process.

You will notice that everyone's Seed and Bloom seasons look different. Some authors walked through loss or disappointment. Others navigated major life transitions, rebuilding, or rediscovery. Even with the differences, one thing is consistent. Each woman leaned into who God was for her during that time. The names chosen for their pages reflect that. They point to His protection, His peace, His faithfulness, His guidance, His strength, His restoration, and His love.

You have seen their stories. What you will see here is the foundation beneath their stories. These scriptures were prayed, repeated, returned to, and held close when life was uncertain. Many of these verses shaped the parts of their journey that were too personal to write in a chapter. Sometimes a single verse does more work in a person's heart than pages of explanation, and that is what this section offers you.

As you read through these Seed and Bloom scriptures, take your time. You may recognize a name of God that speaks directly to where you are, or you may discover a new one that meets you in a way you did not expect. Allow whatever stands out to land with you. Let it be personal.

Whether you are in a Seed season trying to stay grounded or you are stepping into a Bloom season and beginning to see things come together, we hope this section gives you something steady to hold on to. These are the scriptures and the revelations of who God was for us when life was stretching us and shaping us.

This is the Word behind our stories.
This is the God who met us in every season.
When you know who He is, you can bloom well because your roots are secure.

Jehovah JIREH

THE GOD WHO PROVIDES AND RESTORES

Anisia Ferguson

Seed Scripture

"For I know the thoughts that I think toward you, saith the Lord, thoughts of peace, and not of evil, to give you an expected end." –*Jeremiah 29:11*

In my darkest moments, when my mind felt fragile and my heart felt overwhelmed, God revealed Himself to me as Jehovah Jireh, the God who provides what you need exactly when you need it. I was buried under pain, confusion, and disappointment, but this promise became my lifeline. Jehovah Jireh reminded me that I was not forgotten and that my suffering was not random and provided me with what I needed most. He provided peace for my anxiety, hope for my despair, and stability for my unraveling. Although I was broken, it was this scripture that kept me from falling apart.

In the past I used to think this provision was only monetary. However, it was during that time I learnt that Jehovah Jireh does not just provide money or resources. He also provides clarity, strength, comfort, and purpose. Even when your situation looks chaotic, His plan remains intact. Trust His provision even when you cannot see His process.

Bloom Scripture

"And I will restore to you the years that the locust hath eaten, the cankerworm, and the caterpiller, and the palmerworm, my great army which I sent among you." – *Joel 2:25*

For years I mourned what I believed I lost—time wasted in a stagnant marriage, years invested in a job that left me feeling unfulfilled, and seasons where my potential felt smothered.

Then God showed up as Jehovah Jireh, not only the God who provides but the God who restores. He told me that nothing surrendered to Him stays wasted. He promised that the years ahead would hold more joy, more growth, and more fulfillment than I ever thought possible. He assured me that He would give me back more than what I thought was stolen.

Jehovah Jireh restores what you cannot replace on your own. Your bloom begins the moment you stop counting losses and start expecting His restoration.

Jehovah ROHI

THE GOD WHO GUIDES AND GROWS YOU

Lisa White

Seed Scripture

"And I say unto you, Ask, and it shall be given you; seek, and ye shall find; knock, and it shall be opened unto you." – Luke 11:9

I chose this scripture because it represents the moments in my life when I finally admitted I needed guidance.

Asking felt humbling, but that is when God revealed Himself to me as Jehovah Rohi, the Lord my Shepherd. He guided my decisions, aligned my steps, and exposed truths I wasn't seeing. Once I asked for direction, He led me with clarity and opened doors I didn't even know to knock on.

Jehovah Rohi shepherded me through some of the toughest choices of my life.

Jehovah Rohi does not leave you guessing. When you ask, He leads. When you seek, He reveals. When you knock, He opens what was always meant for you.

Bloom Scripture

"My brethren, count it all joy when ye fall into divers temptations; Knowing this, that the trying of your faith worketh patience. But let patience have her perfect work, that ye may be perfect and entire, wanting nothing." James 1:2–4

This scripture is meaningful because it helped me understand that Jehovah Rohi was guiding me even through the trials.

Every test developed perseverance. Every setback strengthened my character. Every challenge refined my faith.

Jehovah Rohi wasn't just leading me out of situations. He was growing me through them.

When Jehovah Rohi guides your process, your pain becomes preparation. He uses every trial to make you mature, grounded, and complete.

El ROI

THE GOD WHO SEES AND REDEEMS

Lynieka Drew

Seed Scripture

"They that sow in tears shall reap in joy." – Psalm 126:5

I chose this scripture because during my seed season, I felt unseen, unheard, and overwhelmed. But God revealed Himself to me as El Roi, the God who sees me.

He saw every sacrifice I made. He saw the tears I cried in silence. He saw the pain behind my smile and the strength behind my endurance.

Even when I felt buried, El Roi was watching over me and strengthening my roots.

When El Roi sees you, nothing you endure is wasted. He uses every tear to build the foundation for your bloom.

Bloom Scripture

"For as the earth bringeth forth her bud, and as the garden causeth the things that are sown in it to spring forth; so the Lord God will cause righteousness and praise to spring forth before all the nations." – Isaiah 61:11

In my bloom season, God showed me that every hidden tear and every silent battle had purpose. El Roi not only saw my pain; He redeemed it. He turned misery into ministry, despair into growth, and heartbreak into hope. This scripture reflects the divine orchestration behind my transformation.

El Roi does not just witness your pain. He redeems it. He turns what tried to break you into the very thing that makes you bloom.

El SHADDAI

THE GOD WHO COVERS AND STRENGTHENS

Lynn Peggy McKinney

Seed Scripture

"He shall cover thee with his feathers, and under his wings shalt thou trust: his truth shall be thy shield and buckler." – Psalm 91:4

I chose this verse because during my divorce, I came to know God as El Shaddai, the One who nurtures, protects, and strengthens. That season stripped away every false source of security I had. I felt emotionally exposed, mentally exhausted, and spiritually drained. But El Shaddai covered me in ways I had never experienced before.

He didn't just protect me; He rebuilt me. He steadied my heart, reminded me of who I was, and carried me through moments when I didn't have the strength to carry myself. Under His covering, I relearned discipline, identity, worth, and the quiet confidence that comes from being held by Someone who never fails.

El Shaddai is not distant. He gathers you close. When life falls apart, He becomes your shield, your refuge, and your strength. His covering is not soft; it is unshakeable. When you let El Shaddai shelter you, you discover a security that no person can give and no circumstance can take away.

Bloom Scripture

"The Lord God is my strength, and he will make my feet like hinds' feet, and he will make me to walk upon mine high places." – Habakkuk 3:19

When I entered my Bloom season, the God who once covered me as El Shaddai revealed Himself as the One who strengthens my steps. He didn't just heal my heart; He empowered my walk. He gave me stability in places that once felt shaky and confidence in areas where I used to be unsure.

Like a deer climbing to higher ground, He positioned me on spiritual and emotional heights I could never have reached on my own.

El Shaddai did not just protect me. He elevated me.

When El Shaddai becomes your source, you stop walking in fear. He strengthens your footing, guides your steps, and places you in positions that reflect His hand, not your hurt. You rise because He lifted you.

Jehovah SHALOM

THE GOD WHO BRINGS STILLNESS AND NEWNESS

Michaella Ann Forbes

Seed Scripture

"The Lord will fight for you; you need only to be still." – Exodus 14:14

I chose this verse because it speaks directly to the part of me that used to fight every battle on my own. I depended on my intelligence, my planning, and my ability to "figure it out." But in this season, God introduced Himself to me as Jehovah Shalom, the God of stillness, peace, calm, and clarity. He showed me that stillness is not weakness. Stillness is trust. Stillness is strategy. Stillness is stepping out of the way long enough for Him to do what only He can do. In the quiet, He brought order to the chaos in my mind and peace to the places in my life where I was drowning in my own effort.

Jehovah Shalom fights differently than you do. He wins without forcing, without rushing, and without panic. When you allow Him to lead, your heart settles, your vision sharpens, and your strength returns. His stillness becomes your protection. His peace becomes your direction.

When you pause long enough for Jehovah Shalom to speak, He shows you that His plan is always better than yours.

Bloom Scripture

"Therefore if any man be in Christ, he is a new creature..." – 2 Corinthians 5:17

This scripture reminds me that God never stops creating, and because I am in Him, neither do I. In my Bloom season, I met Jehovah Shalom again, not as the God who calmed me but as the God who made me new. He breathed creativity, renewal, and confidence into me.

As a creative woman, this verse awakened something deep inside of me. It reminded me that I am a reflection of a Creative God, and I am free to evolve as many times as He calls me to.

Jehovah Shalom does more than calm your storms. He restores your identity. He renews your mind. He makes you whole. Even if yesterday was chaotic, He offers you a fresh beginning today.

When you walk with Him, "new" is not an event. It is a lifestyle. He turns your stillness into growth and your surrender into a bloom you never imagined.

Jehovah
NISSI

THE GOD WHO GOES BEFORE ME AND COVERS ME

Raquel Bain

Seed Scripture

"The Lord himself goes before you and will be with you; he will never leave you nor forsake you." – Deuteronomy 31:8

I chose this scripture because it carried me through the years when I felt like I was walking through life alone. I had done everything "right" — honored God, built a family, worked hard — and still found myself divorced, raising two children on my own, and stretching one paycheck to cover every need. Those were seasons when I could have believed I was forgotten.

But that is where God revealed Himself to me as Jehovah Nissi, the One who goes before me and covers me. Even when my strength was gone, He made the money stretch, opened doors I didn't ask for, and steadied me when I was just putting one foot in front of the other.

Jehovah Nissi walks ahead of you, even when life feels unfair and heavy. He covers you in moments you feel abandoned and strengthens you in places you feel empty. You can move forward with confidence knowing you are not building your life alone — He is already in the tomorrow you're afraid of.

Bloom Scripture

"I have loved thee with an everlasting love." – Jeremiah 31:3

This scripture speaks to my Bloom because God used His love to pull me out of the numbness that followed my divorce. For a long time, I functioned without passion, joy, or dreams for myself. But slowly, Jehovah Nissi began covering my heart in a new way.

His love reminded me that divorce did not diminish me. His kindness helped me release shame, reclaim my identity, and believe that there was still more ahead for me than the pain behind me. His covering allowed me to dream again — to think about mentoring other women, rebuilding my life, and stepping into new purpose.

When Jehovah Nissi covers you with His everlasting love, you stop defining yourself by what ended and start rising into who you are becoming. His love gives you permission to breathe again, hope again, and bloom again.

Jehovah SABOATH

THE GOD WHO BRINGS STILLNESS AND NEWNESS

Shiland A. Bosfield

Seed Scripture

"They that sow in tears shall reap in joy. He that goeth forth and weepeth, bearing precious seed, shall doubtless come again with rejoicing, bringing his sheaves with him." – Psalm 126:5–6

I chose this scripture because my seed season was full of tears, but it was also where God introduced Himself as Jehovah Sabaoth, the Lord of Hosts, the God who fights for me.

I kept sowing faith even when I felt empty.

I kept praying even when nothing changed.

I kept believing even when life made no sense.

What felt like breaking was really God's battle strategy. He was fighting for me behind the scenes while I sowed seeds with my tears. Jehovah Sabaoth turned my pain into purpose.

Jehovah Sabaoth sees every tear as a seed. He turns your battles into breakthroughs and your sorrow into a harvest.

Bloom Scripture

"For our light affliction, which is but for a moment, worketh for us a far more exceeding and eternal weight of glory; While we look not at the things which are seen, but at the things which are not seen: for the things which are seen are temporal; but the things which are not seen are eternal." – 2 Corinthians 4:17–18

In my bloom season, God revealed the weight of glory He had been building inside me. Jehovah Sabaoth showed me that the war I survived had a purpose.

The hardships were temporary, but what He produced in me was eternal.

He didn't just let me survive the storm. He strengthened me through it.

When Jehovah Sabaoth fights your battles, your bloom carries glory that lasts far beyond the pain that birthed it.

THE MEET AUTHORS

Anisia Ferguson

Anisia Ferguson was born and raised in Nassau, Bahamas, and now enjoys the quiet beauty of life on Cat Island, which she affectionately calls her place of serenity. A devoted single mother of two, she considers her children her greatest blessings and her constant motivation.

The third of four children born to the late Leon Ferguson and Frances Ferguson, Anisia knew early that teaching was her calling. She earned a Bachelor's degree in Secondary Education with a specialization in Spanish from the College of The Bahamas, now the University of The Bahamas, and later completed a Master's degree in Education from Walden University.

With more than sixteen years of experience in education across multiple levels, she is currently pursuing a doctoral degree in Organizational Leadership and Development with aspirations of becoming a university professor. Her long-term goal is to serve as an agent of positive social change within the Bahamian educational system through leadership, advocacy, and academic influence.

Faith has remained central to Anisia's life. Raised as a Seventh-day Adventist Christian, she has served in Youth, Children's, Women's, and Music Ministry, which remains her favorite. She believes she is closest to God through worship and music, and she often ministers through gospel and inspirational song. Music has carried her through some of the most difficult moments of her life and continues to be one of the ways she strengthens and encourages others.

Anisia's contribution to this anthology reflects a testimony of obedience, resilience, and restoration. Her story explores the tension between worldly expectations and the quiet warnings of the Holy Spirit, the cost of choosing outside of God's will, and the mercy that meets us even in the consequences of disobedience.

She also shares how God used major turning points, including divorce and the loss of a long-term job, not to destroy her, but to realign her and deepen her reliance on Him. Now in what she calls her "restoration years," Anisia is committed to helping other women see their worth in Christ, embrace emotional growth, and learn the strength of waiting on God's timing.

Anchored in Romans 8:28, she lives with confidence that God truly works all things together for good for those who love Him and are called according to His purpose. Her prayer is that her story will encourage at least one woman to choose God's voice over pressure, and to trust that even the hardest seasons can become holy ground.

To connect with Anisia further on social media, scan this code with your mobile device:

Lisa White

Lisa White was born and raised in Nassau, Bahamas, and her life reflects quiet endurance shaped by grace. Her journey has included storms that could have broken her, yet she stands today as living proof that God restores, rebuilds, and makes all things new in His perfect timing.

With more than thirty years of experience in the insurance and banking industries, Lisa is known for her professionalism, resilience, and a heart that has learned to trust God deeply, even when the path ahead was unclear.

For twenty-two years, Lisa was rooted in the Catholic faith. Her spiritual journey shifted profoundly on August 19, 2018, when she walked through the doors of Bahamas Harvest Church and encountered the unmistakable presence of God.

One month later, she joined Starting Point and stepped into a season of awakening and transformation. She later served in ministry and completed Journey 101 by December of that same year. From the beginning, she knew she had found home. God did not simply lead her to a church, but to healing, purpose, and a deeper understanding of her spiritual identity.

Lisa contributes to this anthology through her chapter titled "In His Time," a deeply personal reflection on surrender, redemption, and the beauty of God's timing.

Her writing flows from a place of healing and hard-earned faith, offering hope to those who have ever questioned their worth, their future, or God's plan. She believes no pain is wasted and no season overlooked when placed in the hands of a God who sees the end from the beginning.

Beyond her spiritual calling, Lisa's greatest joy comes from those who call her Mom and Mimi. She is the proud mother of two daughters, Jewel and Janae. Jewel is a gifted chef and visionary entrepreneur leading Food for Thought and Virtual Office, while Janae followed in her footsteps into the banking profession.

Her granddaughter brings added joy, laughter, and light to her life. Lisa takes pride in the strength, confidence, and ambition of her daughters, which reflect the foundation she built through love, resilience, and unwavering devotion.

Among family and friends, Lisa is also known for her gift in the kitchen. Cooking is her love language and a way she nurtures, connects, and brings comfort to others.

Guided by the truth, "What you're not changing, you're choosing," Lisa is passionate about encouraging women to embrace transformation. For her, this anthology is not simply a chapter, but the beginning of a new, spirit-led season marked by courage, purpose, and faith.

To connect with Lisa further on social media, scan this code with your mobile device:

Lynieka Drew

LYNIEKA DREW IS A MOTHER, entrepreneur, and visionary whose life embodies an unshakable balance of faith, family, and purpose.

A seasoned banking professional at an Offshore Bank, Lynieka is known for her precision, discipline, and commitment to excellence, ensuring compliance, operational accuracy, and integrity in every task she undertakes. Her analytical mindset and focused leadership ensure that every task is handled with care and accountability.

As Vice President of her daughter's school PTA Executive Board, Lynieka leads with purpose and collaboration, driving initiatives that strengthen school, family, and community ties.

Beyond the corporate and leadership spheres, she is the founder of three successful ventures: FerGuSons Cleaning Essentials, a supplier of household and commercial cleaning products; Say Cheesecake, a boutique dessert brand loved for its rich, handcrafted cheesecakes; and WeCare Kits, personal care packages that bring comfort and dignity to students and adults alike. She's also a savvy personal shopper who often jokes, *"What's better than doing what you love than with other people's money?"* Each brand showcases her creativity, heart for service, and ability to turn vision into reality. Fearless in her pursuits, she steps out on faith and lets God handle the rest.

Known for her entrepreneurial insight, Lynieka delights in helping others discover their gifts and develop business ideas that align with their purpose.

Faith is the anchor of her life. An active member of Bahamas Harvest Church, she has served in the Starting Point and Groups Ministries and currently contributes to the Singles Ministry strategy team. She also leads small Christian groups that foster growth, faith, and connection.

Her passion for resilience and divine purpose extends to her writing. She is a contributing author to an upcoming anthology on overcoming adversity, featuring her personal chapter, *"Unbroken – Beauty for Ashes,"* inspired by Isaiah 61:3 and the image of the phoenix rising from the ashes.

Lynieka is a devoted mother to LaMarque Jr. and LaMiea, whose growth in faith, academics, and the arts remain her greatest motivation. She affectionately calls them her "Sonshine" and "Mini Me," and every goal she pursues is part of the legacy she's building for them.

Active in community and event planning, Lynieka continues to expand her reach, explore new opportunities, and give back through volunteer service. Her life reflects grace in motion,ambition fueled by faith, creativity guided by order, and strength refined through purpose.

In her downtime, she enjoys music, social media, concerts, travel, and reading recognizing that these moments help her maintain balance, recharge her spirit, and stay grounded.

Her guiding scripture, which grounds every step of her journey, is found in Isaiah 40:31: *"They that wait upon the Lord shall renew their strength; they shall mount up with wings as eagles."*

To connect with Lynieka further on social media, scan this code with your mobile device:

Lynn Peggy McKinney

Lynn Peggy McKinney is a native of Nassau, Bahamas, where she lives as the proud mother of three sons and grandmother of two beautiful granddaughters who inspire her daily. Her faith and family form the foundation of her life, and compassion for others guides every decision she makes.

An avid reader from a young age, Lynn has always found refuge and renewal in books. That lifelong love of learning continues today, with a deep interest in personal development, business strategy, and theology. She believes growth is a lifelong calling and now channels her love of words as a Christian content creator, sharing reflections through blogging and Facebook that encourage and uplift others. Her passion for the written word continues to grow, and she plans to pursue editing as her next professional venture.

An introvert by nature, Lynn has learned that self-care is not selfish, but essential. People often seek her out for wisdom during difficult seasons, and she remains grounded through prayer, devotional time, and Bible study. Nature serves as her sanctuary, whether walking Nassau's shores or sitting beneath the Bahamian sky. Integrity and consistency anchor her faith, as she believes character is revealed not in words, but in how faithfully we show up.

Creativity runs through Lynn's lineage and flows through her hands. Inspired by her mother, a seamstress, and her grandmother, who crafted Bahamian straw baskets, Lynn expresses her creativity through crocheting, sewing, and repurposing everyday items into something beautiful. For her, creativity is a reflection of redemption and the belief that broken things can be made whole again.

Philanthropy holds a special place in Lynn's heart. As a single mother, she experienced the power of generosity firsthand and lives by the principle that we are blessed to be a blessing. Her service journey began in soup kitchen ministry and expanded to children's ministry and mentoring young girls and women, a commitment she continues today.

With more than four decades in the insurance industry, Lynn brings together analytical expertise and deep empathy as she prepares to become a certified life coach and women's empowerment mentor. She holds a business degree from the College of the Bahamas, now the University of the Bahamas, along with certification from the Chartered Insurance Institute in England and the American Embassy's Academy for Women Entrepreneurs. These experiences now shape her entrepreneurial vision, which includes business consulting, family-focused wellness, legacy and wealth planning, resume development, business planning, and authorship support, all centered on helping women rediscover their God-given identity as fearless, free, and wonderfully made.

To connect with Lynn further, scan these codes with your mobile device:

Website

Facebook

Michaella Ann Forbes

MICHAELLA ANN FORBES, WIDELY known as *The Artistic Accountant*, is a dynamic fusion of creativity and financial mastery. A Certified Public Accountant and Chartered Financial Analyst with more than twenty years in the finance profession, she has built a reputation for precision, integrity, and leadership in the world of numbers. Yet her deepest calling has always been rooted in art, storytelling, and human expression.

Michaella believes she is closest to God when she creates, reflecting the nature of the ultimate Creator who designed the heavens, the earth, and everything in between. Though she chose a traditional path in accounting due to her exceptional skill with numbers, the pull toward artistic expression never left her.

Her creative journey reignited in 2009 through the Adult Drama Ministry at Bahamas Harvest Church. That spark led her to audition for The Dundas Centre for the Performing Arts in 2014, where she landed her debut role as "Green" in *For Colored*

Girls. This pivotal moment opened the door to numerous acting and directing opportunities across the community.

As her love for the stage deepened, so did her expansion into writing, producing, and directing. In 2016, she was officially branded *The Artistic Accountant* when she wrote, produced, and directed her original stage play, All of Me, inspired by her own life and spiritual journey. Presented at The Dundas in 2017, the play earned her a Bahamian Icon Award nomination in 2018 and was later requested for special presentations, including the *LIT & Single* series at Bahamas Harvest Church and the 2019 Buttons Bridal Show.

In 2020, Michaella transitioned from stage to film, expanding her artistic portfolio through music videos and her short film Distant, which premiered at the Bahamas International Film Festival. In 2023, following her divorce, Michaella launched A Safe Space, one of the Bahamas' most resonant podcasts. The platform creates room for honest conversations around pain, healing, restoration, and growth, and has quickly gained recognition for its depth, authenticity, and emotional intelligence.

Michaella's entrepreneurial calling expanded again through the creation of Purpose Pulse Coaching, where she guides writers and creative visionaries from page to stage. By blending financial strategy with artistic mastery, she helps clients build authentic, purpose-driven projects with both precision and profitability.

A multi-passionate creator, Michaella embodies the integration of numbers and narrative, structure and spirit. Through her leadership, mentorship, and creative work, she empowers others not just to tell their stories, but to steward them with intention, excellence, and faith.

To connect with Michaella further, scan these codes with your mobile device:

Website

Facebook

Raquel Bain

RAQUEL BAIN IS A Nassau, Bahamas native whose voice is rooted in faith, realism, and the kind of resilience that is built quietly over time. A finance professional by training and a writer by calling, Raquel is known for combining strong stewardship with a deeply compassionate heart. She believes that strength is not only spiritual, but practical. It is the ability to keep building, keep believing, and keep showing up, even when life does not look like the story you expected.

Professionally, Raquel serves as a Finance Lead at an international company, where she brings excellence, integrity, and strategic clarity to her work. Her financial discipline has shaped not only her career, but also her personal journey.

Through seasons of transition and rebuilding, she learned that wisdom, planning, and patience are often the tools God uses to sustain us. In her chapter, she shares how stewardship became a form of worship, and how maturity is often revealed through structure, responsibility, and intentional living.

Raquel is the devoted mother of two teenagers, Micah and Mikayla, and much of her life is centered on creating stability, safety, and opportunity for them. Her story explores themes of identity, belonging, and family, including growing up without her biological father present, the gift of a loving stepfather, and the unspoken questions that can follow a child into adulthood. Her journey through divorce and single parenting also includes navigating her son's autism diagnosis, a season that stretched her emotionally, spiritually, and financially, while revealing God's faithfulness in unexpected ways.

Faith remains central to Raquel's life. She is an active member of Bahamas Harvest Church, where community, spiritual growth, and accountability have played a key role in her healing and renewal. S

he is also passionate about service and mentorship, believing that shared wisdom can steady others in difficult seasons. In 2023, she joined the Kiwanis Club of Fort Montague, where she now serves as Public Relations Chair, helping to support outreach initiatives that strengthen families and uplift children across her community.

A lifelong reader and a proud daughter who honors her mother, Veronica, Raquel dreamed of writing for more than a decade before returning to her first love, the written word. Her debut contribution in Roses in Bloom, a #1 bestselling anthology on

Amazon, marks the beginning of a new season of authorship. Raquel writes what she has lived, and she shares her story to remind women that growth is often quiet, healing is often gradual, and God is still at work in the middle of becoming.

To connect with Raquel further on social media, scan this code with your mobile device:

Shiland Bosfield

Shiland Amanda Bosfield was born and raised in Nassau, The Bahamas, with deep family roots in Crooked Island. She is a selfless and devoted mother to her three children, Rasheed, Shalia, and Safia. She is also a loyal friend whose bright and infectious personality lights up every environment she enters. Anchored by God's love, she has spent more than 20 years in customer service, bringing joy to every interaction and extending kindness to people from all walks of life.

Throughout her career, Shiland has served at two well-known hotel brands and a major airline. She earned multiple Employee of the Month and Employee of the Year awards. Her peers affectionately call her "The Friendly Skies Ambassador," a reflection of her exceptional customer service and the lasting smiles she leaves with customers.

Shiland's life has included seasons marked by domestic violence, heartbreak, and three divorces. These experiences required her to rebuild her life many times. By the grace of God, she rose after each hardship with renewed strength and deeper intention. Her healing journey taught her the importance of honest self-reflection. She realized that true restoration required her to acknowledge her emotions, confront her pain, and work through it in order to emerge whole, healthy, and renewed.

Today, she is devoted to redirecting the love and care she once misplaced back into herself. She practices purposeful self-care and prioritizes rest, reflection, and rejuvenation. She enjoys spa days, pampering, and peaceful moments that allow her to honor her body, mind, and spirit as sacred gifts from God.

A proud member of Bahamas Harvest Church since 2013, Shiland believes that serving others is an important part of building God's Kingdom. Since 2024, she has served as a small-group leader with a special passion for supporting women who are recovering from broken relationships and rebuilding their confidence through God's unconditional love.

She enjoys singing, gardening, traveling, exploring new cultures, and watching crime-based investigative programs. She also has an appreciation for a wide range of music including Bahamian rhythms, jazz, classical music, and live performances.

Rooted deeply in her faith, Shiland found healing through prayer, therapy, and a renewed relationship with Jesus Christ. She is committed to nurturing her joy, cultivating her growth, and strengthening the relationships that matter most.

Her contribution to this anthology reflects her belief that with God, even the hardest seasons can lead to restoration and renewed strength. She hopes her story encourages women who are facing difficult chapters and reminds them that those who wait upon the Lord will find new strength.

To connect with Shiland further on social media, scan this code with your mobile device:

IF YOU NEED HELP

If You Need Help

If you are reading this and find yourself in a season of emotional strain, financial instability, or the silent weight of a relationship that has wounded more than it has healed, you are not alone. Every woman in these pages reached a moment where she had to whisper the hardest truth: *I need help.* That truth is not weakness. It is wisdom. And it is the beginning of rebuilding.

Start with people or places that feel safe.

A trusted friend. A spiritual mentor. A therapist. A support group. A women's ministry leader. Safety is not just about where you go, it's about who will honor your story without judgment.

If any type of abuse, manipulation, or distress is involved, reach out sooner rather than later.

You deserve clarity, support, and practical guidance. Many women suffer quietly because they don't know what help looks like or where to find it. Here are options to consider:

- Local women's shelters or crisis centers that provide

confidential support, counseling, and emergency planning.

- Licensed counselors or therapists trained in trauma, grief, or relationship recovery.
- Family law attorneys who can advise you on your rights, even before you make any decisions.
- Financial advisors or nonprofit credit counseling agencies who can help you understand your financial picture, especially if money has been used as a tool of control.
- Faith-based support communities where you can process your pain without shame and rebuild your identity with spiritual grounding.

Speak the Word of God Over Your Life

In moments when your strength feels scattered and your hope feels thin, **speak the Word of God. Out loud. Over your home, your mind, your children, your finances, and your future.** Not because Scripture is magic, but because **it is truth. It is power. It is life.**

Declare God's promises even when you cannot yet see the path:

- *"When my heart is overwhelmed, lead me to the rock that is higher than I."*
- *"The Lord is my shepherd; I shall not want."*

- *"No weapon formed against me shall prosper."*
- *"God is within her; she will not fail."*

God responds to faith, even faith that trembles. **Open your mouth and declare what He says, not what your situation says.** He will steady you. He will strengthen you. He will make a way.

Your job is to take the **first step you know how,** reach out, tell someone, ask for help, pray, breathe, move. God meets you in motion.**A**

Spiritual Resource for Women Walking Through Hard Seasons

For women seeking a faith-anchored space to heal, **Bahamas Harvest Church** is a powerful resource. They offer:

- Online and in-person services
- Counseling and pastoral care
- Support groups
- Teachings and community gatherings designed to strengthen the heart, restore identity, and provide spiritual stability through difficult seasons

Whether you are local to The Bahamas or joining from anywhere in the world, their ministry provides a compassionate and practical covering for women needing guidance, community, and prayer.

You Don't Have to Walk Through This Alone

As the women in *Roses in Bloom* have shown, healing is not a straight line. It is a journey made possible by courage, community, and grace. Reach for help. Receive it. And remind yourself that survival is not your whole story, *blooming is.*

Gentle Disclaimer

This section is offered for encouragement and general guidance. It is not a substitute for professional counseling, legal advice, or emergency support. If you are in immediate danger or experiencing severe emotional distress, please seek assistance from licensed professionals, crisis hotlines, or local emergency services. Your safety and well-being matter.

Thank you for investing your time and heart into this book.

One of the greatest ways you can continue the impact is by sharing your thoughts in a review, it helps this message reach those who need it most!

Scan here to leave a review on Amazon
(even if you didn't purchase from there!)

Made in the USA
Coppell, TX
20 January 2026

68522725R00174